Anne Rice

CALLED OUT OF DARKNESS

Anne Rice is the author of twenty-nine books. She lives in Rancho Mirage, California.

www.annerice.com

CALLED OUT OF DARKNESS

A Spiritual Confession

ANNE RICE

ANCHOR BOOKS

A Division of Random House, Inc.

New York

FIRST ANCHOR BOOKS EDITION, MARCH 2010

Grateful acknowledgment is made to Curtis Brown, Ltd., for permission
to reprint an excerpt from "The Tale of Custard, the Dragon" by Ogden Nash,
copyright © 1936 by Ogden Nash (originally published in *Child Life* magazine in 1936).

The Library of Congress has cataloged the Knopf edition as follows:
Rice, Anne, [date]
Called out of darkness : a spiritual confession / by Anne Rice.
p. cm.
1. Rice, Anne, [date] 2. Spiritual biography—United States.
3. Women novelists, American—20th century—Biography.
4. Rice, Anne, [date]—Homes and haunts—Louisiana—New Orleans.
5. Spiritual life, Catholic Church. I. Title.
PS3568.I265Z4626 2008
813'.54—dc22
2008020192

Anchor ISBN: 978-0-307-38848-3

Book design by Virginia Tan

www.anchorbooks.com

146122990

Out of the depths have I cried unto thee, O LORD.

Lord, hear my voice: let thine ears be attentive to the voice of my supplications.

If thou, LORD, shouldst mark iniquities, O Lord, who shall stand?

But there is forgiveness with thee, that thou mayest be feared.

I wait for the LORD, my soul doth wait, and in his word do I hope.

My soul waiteth for the Lord more than they that watch for the morning: I say, more than they that watch for the morning.

—From Psalm 130
The King James Version

CALLED OUT OF DARKNESS

I

THIS BOOK IS ABOUT FAITH IN GOD.

For more than twenty centuries, Christianity has given us dazzling works of theology, yet it remains a religion in which the heart is absolutely essential to faith.

The appeal of Jesus Christ was first and foremost to the heart.

The man knocked on his back on the Road to Damascus experienced a transformation of the heart. St. Francis of Assisi, giving away all of his clothes as he turned to follow Christ, was reflecting a decision of the heart. Mother Teresa founded her world-famous order of nuns because of a decision of the heart.

The immensity of these figures finds an imperfect student in me, but not an inattentive one.

I want to tell, as simply as I can—and nothing with me as

a writer has ever really been simple—the story of how I made my decision of the heart.

So here is the story of one path to God.

The story has a happy ending because I have found the Transcendent God both intellectually and emotionally. And complete belief in Him and devotion to Him, no matter how interwoven with occasional fear and constant personal failure and imperfection, has become the true story of my life.

If this path to God is an illusion, then the story is worthless. If the path is real, then we have something here that may matter to you as well as to me.

2

BEFORE I CAN DESCRIBE how I returned to faith, at the age of fifty-seven, I want to describe how I learned about God as a child.

What strikes me now as most important about this experience is that it preceded reading books. Christians are People of the Book, and our religion is often described as a Religion of the Book. And for two thousand years, all that we believe has been handed down in texts.

But no doubt many children learned about God as I did—from my mother and from the experience of church which had little or nothing directly to do with knowing how to read.

Over the years, I turned out to be a consistently poor reader, and I don't think I ever read a novel for pleasure until I was in the sixth grade. Even in my college years, I was a poor reader and, in fact, couldn't major in English because I could not read the amounts of Chaucer or Shakespeare assigned in the classes. I graduated with a bachelor of arts degree in political science, principally because I could understand the historic background I received for political ideas through good lectures.

I was twenty-seven before I began to make up an undergraduate degree in English, and thirty-one before I received a master's in English. Even then I read so slowly and poorly that I took my master's orals on three authors, Shakespeare, Virginia Woolf, and Ernest Hemingway, without having read all of their works. I couldn't possibly read all of their works.

The reason I'm emphasizing this is because I believe that what we learn through reading is essentially different from what we learn in other ways. And my concept of God came through the spoken words of my mother, and also the intensely beautiful experiences I had in church.

It's important to stress here that my earliest experiences involved beauty; my strongest memories are of beautiful things I saw, things which evoked such profound feeling in me that I often felt pain.

In fact I remember my early childhood as full of beauty, and no ugly moment from that time has any reality for me. The beauty is the song of those days.

I vividly remember knowing about God, that He loved us, made us, took care of us, that we belonged to Him; and I remember loving Jesus as God; and praying to Him and to His Blessed Mother, the Virgin Mary, when I was very small.

I can't really associate any one image with Jesus because

there were so many around me, from small highly sentimental holy pictures, which we treasured at home, to magnificent images of Jesus in St. Alphonsus Church.

I'll describe the church in a minute, as it takes considerable describing, but first I want to mention a small place where we went often to pray. This was the Chapel of Our Mother of Perpetual Help on Third and Prytania streets, a consecrated Catholic chapel with a tabernacle and an altar, in which Mass was celebrated every day. The chapel was a huge room inside an old Garden District mansion, set in spacious gardens, that was also a high school.

My mother had graduated from this high school many years before, and I recall going to a garden party on the grounds when I was a little child. The building itself was impressive, with a central doorway, floor-length windows on the front and on both sides, and colonnettes along the front porch that held up the porch above.

Much later in life—during the 1990s—when I was a well-known author, I actually bought this building, as it had tremendous meaning for me. Not only had my mother gone to school there, but my aunts and cousins had gone to school there as well. Some cousins had been married in the chapel. And my strongest religious memories were centered on this place. The story of that purchase and what it meant requires a book, and indeed I wrote a novel using the building as a key backdrop, but that is not my concern just now.

This is what it was like in the 1940s to go to the Chapel of Our Mother of Perpetual Help.

We left our house at St. Charles and Philip, and walked

up the avenue, under the oaks, and almost always to the slow roar of the passing streetcars, and rumble of traffic, then crossed over into the Garden District, a very special neighborhood filled with immense Greek Revival–style homes, many of which had been built before the Civil War. This was an immediate plunge into a form of quiet, because though traffic did move steadily on Prytania Street, it was nothing as loud as the traffic of the avenue. The oaks were bigger and more ancient, and the enormous houses with their Corinthian or Doric columns were monuments in themselves. Everywhere there were flowers. Purple lantana and ice blue plumbago burst through the pickets of black iron fences, and beyond in the more groomed gardens grew the flowers I associated with rich people: multi-petaled camellias and gorgeously defined roses in black beds. It was fine to pick the soft fragrant lantana, and the bunches of plumbago. The finer flowers one left alone.

It was often evening when we made this short walk, and I remember the pavements as clearly as I remember the cicadas singing in the trees. The pavements varied; some were herringbone brick, very dark, uneven, and often trimmed in velvet green moss. Other sidewalks were purple flagstone, just like the purple flagstones of our own front yard. Even the rare stretches of raw cement were interesting because the cement had broken and buckled in so many places over the roots of the giant magnolias and the oaks.

The walk was two and a half blocks.

The chapel stood behind a high black picket fence with its gate permanently open, and a short flight of white marble steps led up to the white marble porch. I don't recall the chapel ever being locked.

The sky during these trips was often bloodred, or purple, and the trees were so thick that one could only see hundreds of fragments of the sky amid clusters of darkening leaves. The color of the sky seemed to me to be connected with the song of the cicadas, and the drowsy shadows playing everywhere on the margins of what was visible, and the distinct feel of the humid air. Even in winter the air was moist, so that the world itself seemed to be pulsing around us, enfolding us, holding us as we moved through it.

The chapel had an immense and ornate doorway.

Immediately on entering, one smelled the wax of the flickering candles, and the lingering incense from the Tuesday night benediction service and from the daily or Sunday Mass.

These fragrances were associated in my mind with the utter quiet of the chapel, the glow of the candlelight, and the faces of the tall plaster saints that surrounded us as we moved up the aisle.

We went right past the many rows of dark wooden pews on either side, up to the Communion railing, which I think was white marble, and there we knelt on the leather-cushioned step as we said our prayers. We laid down there the flowers we'd picked on our walk. I think my mother told us that Mr. Charlie, who took care of the chapel, would put these flowers in some proper place.

The great altar against the back wall, just beyond us, was a masterpiece of white and gilt plasterwork, and the altar proper, the place where Mass was said, was always covered with an ornate lace-bordered white cloth.

In a long horizontal glass case in the lower body of the altar, there sat a long series of small plaster statues around a table making up the Last Supper, with Our Lord in the center, and six Apostles on either side. I knew this was Jesus there at the table, facing us. And in later years, I came to realize the figures were arranged in imitation of Da Vinci's *Last Supper*. It was detailed and artful and complete.

The Body and Blood of Jesus were in the golden tabernacle on the altar above. This was the Blessed Sacrament. A candle burning in a red glass lamp nearby told us that the Blessed Sacrament was there. This was called the sanctuary light.

On account of this Presence of Our Lord in the chapel, we moved with reverence, whispering if we had to speak, and kneeling as was proper. This chapel required all the same respect as any large Catholic church.

I remember the gold tabernacle had a concave front, and carved doors. The tabernacle was set in a lavish plaster edifice that included small white columns, but the details are now gone from my mind.

We said our prayers as we knelt there. We paid our "visit." And we left as quietly as we had come.

I don't remember being particularly puzzled by these truths, that Our Lord was in the tabernacle, in the form of bread, which was in fact His Body and Blood. I just remember knowing it. He was most definitely there. He was splendidly and miraculously there. He was also completely accessible. We talked to Him. We told Him our prayers and our thoughts.

I was accustomed to all this before I could talk or ask a question, and I was as certain that Jesus was there as I was that the streetcars passed our house. I was nourished on the complexity of this, and I suppose I felt quite gently filled with these ideas.

Above the tabernacle, in an ornate frame, was an exotic and dark golden picture of Our Mother of Perpetual Help— the Virgin with the Boy Jesus in her lap. This was indeed a distinct image, quite different from anything else in the chapel, and I don't recall ever asking why.

Years later I discovered it was a Russian icon, and that was the reason for its unusual style. What I remember knowing when I was little was that Mary was our Mother as well as the Mother of Jesus, and that in this picture, the Boy Jesus had come to her with a broken sandal, seeking her help.

A long time later, I learned the story of the picture—that the Boy Jesus had run to His Mother in fear. Angels on either side of Him, quite visible in the icon, had frightened Him by revealing to Him the cross on which He would one day die, and the nails that would be driven through His hands. These angels hovered in the air with these terrible instruments. Being only a boy, Jesus had run to His Mother for comfort, and with a sorrowful face she embraced Him and sought to give Him the solace He so badly needed.

As a little child, I saw all these elements and I understood them in a less narrative way. There was the Child leaning tenderly on His Mother, and there was she, His eternal comfort, and, yes, there were the angels holding the emblems of what Jesus would one day undergo.

That Jesus had been crucified, had died, and had risen from the dead was completely understood. One had to look no farther than the Stations of the Cross along the walls to see that story acted out step by step.

These Stations, which were square paintings, each richly colored and detailed, were vivid and realistic in style, as was every other image in the church.

To me they looked interesting and were irresistibly pretty. There was nothing exotic or abstract about them as there was with the icon.

In each picture, Our Lord was serene and infinitely patient, a tall handsome man with long soft brown hair. We felt an immediate sadness when we thought about what Jesus had suffered. But Jesus was now quite beyond all suffering, and what He had suffered, He had suffered on earth among people, and He had suffered it for us.

The other important elements in the chapel were the life-size statues, each painted in vivid color. They stood on pedestals along the walls.

My favorite was the statue of the Infant Jesus of Prague. This was the Boy Jesus, again, in lavish gold-trimmed robes, and wearing a golden crown on his blond head. He had a radiant and chubby face—picture a four-year-old—and He held a world globe with a cross atop it in His left hand, while He raised two fingers in blessing with His right. He stared forward with wise and clear blue eyes. I knew this was Jesus as He had appeared to someone, but I don't recall knowing the name of the saint who saw the vision, only that it had of course happened in Prague. The way we spoke of this image was like a little song: TheInfantJesusofPrague.

Another statue I remember from the chapel was that of St. Thérèse, The Little Flower, a beautiful Carmelite nun, who had died when she was a young woman. Her oval face, in its white wimple, was perfect sweetness, and she had a half smile on her faintly rouged lips. She stood gazing invitingly at us, innocent, timelessly happy, resplendent in her Carmelite robes of beige and white, under her long black veil. In her hands, she held a crucifix, but she also held a huge bouquet of roses. She was known as The Little Flower, and this too was always spoken as a tiny song. The Little Flower had been in life a modest and simple girl, nothing as grand as St. Teresa of Avila, or St. Rita or St. Joseph, or St. Anthony of Padua, but The Little Flower worked miracles all the time. Sometimes when this saint worked a miracle, the person found himself enveloped in the scent of roses. I pictured a shower of rose petals when I thought of such a moment. The Little Flower had said that she wanted to spend her Heaven doing good on earth.

I talked all the time back then to The Little Flower. . . . And I talked to St. Joseph, the foster father of Jesus. I talked to the Blessed Mother unendingly, and I talked to Jesus all the time.

Even as a quiet little girl, I knew perfectly well that none of the statues or pictures of Jesus was Jesus. These were all symbols of Jesus. That's why you could have Jesus being crucified in a picture, or sitting at table at the Last Supper or

Jesus as a beautiful little boy. You could talk to the Child Jesus or you could talk to Jesus on the cross, or Jesus in the tabernacle. It was all Jesus. Jesus was beyond time, and Jesus was actually beyond place. Yes, He was in the tabernacle, but He was everywhere, too. You could close your eyes and talk to Him in the middle of a sidewalk if you wanted to. Jesus heard you whenever you spoke to Him. And Jesus saw you all the time whether you wanted Him to, or not.

The concepts were not puzzling and they were part of life.

Jesus was God. Jesus was part of the Holy Trinity along with God the Father, and the Holy Spirit. God made the world, which meant that Jesus made the world. The Little Flower's statue wasn't The Little Flower. St. Anthony's statue was not St. Anthony. All these beings were in Heaven, but there was no definite boundary separating them from us. Anybody in Heaven could listen to your prayers and help you, if you asked for help. The Virgin Mary and the saints were close to God and they could "intercede" for you. There came with these concepts a whole slew of interesting words, and those interesting words were part of the songs and prayers of the faith that I heard from the time I was born.

My talking to Jesus was intimate. Though we knew the Our Father, and we knew the Hail Mary, we spoke to God in our own words. In fact, in those earliest memories, I don't recall rote prayers.

The reason I've taken so long to describe this world in detail is because it is the world I knew before I was taught to read.

The knowledge of God, His Divine Son, and His saints

was entirely iconic. And as scientists tell us, what we learn through pictures or icons is strikingly different from what we learn through the written word. The brain receives this information in a unique way. Learning from books is something else altogether.

My faith in God was strong before I ever saw a page of catechism, and certainly before I ever saw a page of the Bible. It wasn't as yet connected with stories from the Bible.

But no document I later read, including the Bible, really changed my concept of God, or my trust in Him, or how much I liked to think about Him. And trust in God was probably the first real relationship to Him that I had. True love of Him was my intention. That was expected. But trust was what the little child in me knew. We lived and breathed as God's children in God's glorious world.

Intermingled with my religious experiences at this time were preliterate aesthetic experiences which left a lasting mark.

For example, I remember having an internal gallery of pictorial images for words before I knew how to spell. Now only one shines bright in memory, the image for the word "Anna Mae" which was the name of my aunt. Actually her full name was Sister Mary Immaculate and she was a Sister of Mercy, a nurse, working at old Mercy Hospital on the river. But we called her Aunt Anna Mae, and every time I heard her name I saw a particular basket of flowers. I still see a basket of flowers when I say her name. Unfortunately, all the other mental images I had are gone now, replaced by the alphabetic letters I learned for these words and names when I learned to read. Only the memory of the richness remains—that words had distinct and fascinating shapes, shapes I liked to see when I said the words.

I also remember responding in highly specific ways to automobiles that passed on St. Charles Avenue. This was the 1940s. Some cars looked like long beetles; others were hump-backed. Others were snub-nosed; all had visual personality. This characterizing of things in terms of personality also left me when I learned to read. But at this early point, when faith in God was planted in me, fascination with shape and texture consumed me. Everywhere I turned I saw things that begged for tributes or descriptions which I couldn't articulate at the time.

Let me describe a few of these experiences because they are so completely interwoven with faith.

One time my mother took us to a convent. I don't remember which convent or why we went or what we did. But when we left it, we walked down a long dark brick side-walk, banked by a row of tall flowering trees. The blossoms on the trees were pink and a shower of pink blossoms had descended on the bricks so that this was a path of petals on which we walked. I remember thinking, tiny child that I was, that this was so incredibly beautiful that it hurt me. I wanted never to lose this beauty, and I must think about that side-walk about once a month. The bricks were reddish brown, of course, and the petals made up a carpet of soft, fragile flutter-ing color. I vaguely recall looking back at this over my shoul-der, not wanting to leave it. The trees might have been crape myrtle trees.

Here's another experience. One afternoon, I knelt on a chair, looking out the screened window of the "middle bedroom" of our house.

The middle bedroom was my favorite bedroom, not only because it had a black fireplace and a black mantelpiece, and three doors, making it somewhat of a passageway, but because it had the view from this window to which I'd brought a chair. Kneeling on the chair, with my elbows on the window, I could gaze for long periods at the house across Philip Street.

This was a magnificent Greek Revival house with upper and lower porches, and a long flank that ran back the block. What made it beautiful to me, however, was a giant pecan tree that sheltered this entire stretch of street, and the purple wisteria vine that bloomed along the brick wall of the garden of this house. I remember wanting desperately to possess the beauty of the wisteria, the clusters of fragile purple blossoms that shivered in the wind, but nevertheless looked like bunches of purple grapes.

When the breezes blew, this huge pecan tree danced in the breeze, and the soft air came through the screen window into the house. I stared at that wisteria vine, loving it, wanting to have it forever. And like the petal-strewn walk, I think of it all the time. It lives and breathes in me, that vine and that wall, and beyond it the high walls of the old beige-colored house.

The house was rich and expensive. A mysterious family lived there, people about whom I knew nothing except that they were named the Rosenthals. After the Rosenthals came the Episcopal bishop, and after that I do not know.

It was the stuff of dreams that I might one day live in such an august house. The fact is I did, decades later, come to live in such a house on a different corner only a few blocks away. And one of the things I did then was to have built for the back of the property a long and beautiful and old-fashioned brick wall. A wonderful craftsman named Rob Newman built the wall, and I suspect no one today knows that the wall is not one hundred years old.

In those early years, all around me I saw things that shaped my perceptions and my longings. I'd stop to look at the Greek columns of the houses against the passing clouds. All up and down St. Charles Avenue there were houses of impressive detail and overwhelming size.

In the evenings, when we would walk along the avenue— and we did this all the time—I loved to look at the cut-glass doors of these houses, and the way the light sparkled in the cut glass. I called them "crystal doors." They were burning and shining in the night. And they had about them an air of mystery because I imagined the interior rooms beyond them were as magnificent as these doors.

On Hallowe'en we went trick-or-treating in the depths of the Garden District. One such door opened, and a tall man stood in a high-ceilinged hallway, on a shining floor, offering us candies in a huge silver bowl. I was hungry to see the secrets of the house in which he lived. I think he was a butler, but I wasn't sure.

These things sound too ordinary as I describe them. They had an air of enchantment. So did the many churches we visited in those days, including the vast Holy Name of Jesus

Church at Loyola University with its forest of soaring columns and white marble statues; and the Jesuit Church downtown with its golden onion domes on the altar and the rich ironwork of its pews.

There was a grotto in those days adjacent to the Jesuit Church, a long stone chamber filled with high thin tapers burning away.

Everywhere I turned, I was assaulted by the sensuous and the atmospheric, and the beautiful. I don't recall ugliness or shabbiness, and I don't recall anything dark or unpleasant. The fabric is unbroken.

Our walks along the avenue to Audubon Park, our trips downtown to the museum called the Cabildo, our rides on the St. Charles streetcar with the windows open to the breeze, even playing in the yard amid the ivy and the wild rosebushes, or venturing up the block past many different types of houses, all this seems part of the same tapestry.

For example, at the end of our block, a Rose of Montana vine had gone wild over the telephone pole and the telephone wires and I loved to look at the arching pink flowers of that lively vine. I loved the green strips of grass that bordered every sidewalk. I never stopped falling in love with particular trees.

On the way to the butcher shop on Baronne Street, two blocks behind our house, we had to pass a long open drainage ditch lined with willow trees, and this seemed to me to be the loveliest of streams.

If there was any ugliness or shabbiness it was perhaps connected with the smaller more crowded houses on Carondelet

Street around the block from our house, and I think what I disliked about this stretch was the complete absence of trees. I'm not sure.

Ceremonies of the church were also part of this tapestry, and those I most distinctly remember took place in the chapel I've described. Daily Mass was extremely interesting because the priest wore vestments of watered taffeta with thick embroidery, and even the altar boy wore a lovely white lace-trimmed surplice over his black robe.

The priest said the Mass in Latin, facing away from us, and moved back and forth across the altar as he consulted an enormous book.

The altar boy rang small golden bells at the moment of the Consecration when the priest spoke in Latin the words of Our Lord from the Last Supper, "This is my body. . . . This is my blood." This was a moment of spectacular importance and utter silence, but then the whole church was silent during the daily Mass. Nevertheless at the moment of the Consecration the miracle of Christ coming into the bread on the altar was being enacted or repeated, and we bowed our heads and said our most personal and emotional prayers.

"Jesus, you are here." It was that sort of intimate whisper. "Lord, you are coming to us." "Lord, I am not worthy that thou shouldst come to me."

Our feelings were those of immense gratitude and wonder. We believed in this miracle as we believed that streetcars passed our house, or that rain fell in great soft glimmering sheets in the afternoons.

One key church service dominates all others except for the Mass. Every Tuesday night, in the chapel, as well as in the main churches of our parish, there was a novena service to Our Mother of Perpetual Help.

Strictly speaking, a novena is a series of nine services devoted to one cause. But most churches had weekly novena services, and how and when you went to nine in a row was your call.

We loved to go to this service. There was no air-conditioning anywhere in those days, except in certain drugstores, and on summer nights the floor-length windows of the chapel were open on all sides. The evening hummed with cicadas.

The chapel was filled with electric light. The priest and the altar boy presided. And usually there were some hundred people or so crowding the dark wooden pews.

I no longer remember the order of the service. I remember what took place.

Benediction was part of it, a ceremony in which the priest removed the white Host of the Blessed Sacrament from the tabernacle, put it into a round glass compartment in the center of a golden monstrance—a one-legged stand with golden rays emanating out from the glass compartment like rays of the sun. Incense was liberally used during this ceremony, with the priest taking the smoking incense holder from the altar boy, and swinging it gently on its chain back and forth to fill the church with the thick delicious perfume.

The priest was attired especially for this ceremony in a gorgeous robe and a small shawl, which was sometimes a bit crooked when the priest knelt before the monstrance—and the Blessed Sacrament—to lead us in prayer.

The hymns we sang before the Blessed Sacrament every

Tuesday night have left perhaps the most indelible impression on me of any music I ever heard before or since. It's this way with many Catholics of my generation. There is a particular love of those two hymns.

Both were in Latin. The first was the most solemn in tone:

> *O Salutaris Hostia,*
> *Quae caeli pandis ostium,*
> *Bella premunt hostilia,*
> *Da robur, fer auxilium.*

This was sung out with a tender tone of appeal, and again a sense of gratitude, a sense of trust. This was Our Lord in the Blessed Sacrament, this was a special moment of adoration, and one gave oneself to it with one's entire heart.

I don't recall caring much about the English meaning of this hymn. The meaning was in the tone and the sound.

The second hymn was sung with positive vigor. The chapel rocked.

> *Tantum ergo Sacramentum*
> *Veneremur cernui:*
> *Et antiquum documentum*
> *Novo cedat ritui.*
> *Praestet fides supplementum*
> *Sensuum defectui*
>
> *Genitori, Genitoque*
> *Laus et jubilatio:*
> *Salus, honor, virtus quoque*

Sit et benedictio:
Procedenti ab utroque
Compar sit laudatio,

Amen.

The hymn was great fun to sing and it reached its highest emotional pitch and most swinging rhythm with the words *Genitori, Genitoque!*—which happen to mean "To the Everlasting Father, and the Son who reigns on high" or so *The Baltimore Book of Prayers* tells me. But to repeat, the words didn't matter in those early days. The sentiment, the sense of the sacred, the sense of the splendid opportunity, were all embodied in the tones and the music.

There were some churches that sang the Tantum Ergo in a more solemn manner, but that wasn't for us in our church or chapel. We bore with it when we attended services in those parishes.

Today one can buy recordings of these ancient hymns, and if you give such a recording to a Catholic of my generation, you can move that person to tears. If you know an old-guard Catholic who's dying, a recording of these hymns may be one of the best gifts you can give that person.

But these recordings are made by large disciplined choirs. They don't really express the enthusiasm, or the conviviality of the services of my time in which people stood or knelt belting out these Latin words in homage to the Divine. Let me stress again: a translation of the hymn wasn't necessary. In fact, we had the translation handy on cards that were given out in the church. What mattered was that through the singing itself we were connecting with the Divine.

The prayer said at this service was called the Divine Praises.

Blessed be God.
Blessed be His holy name.
Blessed be Jesus Christ, true God and true man.
Blessed be the Name of Jesus.
Blessed be His most Sacred Heart.
Blessed be Jesus in the Most Holy Sacrament of the Altar.
Blessed be the great Mother of God, Mary most holy.
Blessed be her holy and Immaculate Conception.
Blessed be the name of Mary, Virgin and Mother.
Blessed be St. Joseph, her most chaste Spouse.
Blessed be God in His Angels and in His Saints.

This was of course a chant, and as a chant it had a lulling effect on us as we heard it or repeated it. The litanies that were said to the Blessed Virgin had the same effect. They were in English, and the priest would address the Virgin title by title, after each of which we would say, "Pray for us." The titles were mysterious and intriguing: Virgin Most Faithful; Mirror of Justice; Seat of Wisdom; Cause of Our Joy; Spiritual Vessel; Vessel of Honor; Singular Vessel of Devotion; Mystical Rose; Tower of David; Tower of Ivory; House of Gold. There were about five times that many titles.

As we knelt participating in this litany we were indeed lulled into a trancelike quiet, meditating on what the words might mean, or merely addressing the Virgin Mary, talking to her, giving our hearts to her under all these many names, and praying for her to intercede with her Divine Son for us and help us.

The effect of almost all prayer, whether during Mass, or during a novena service or during a benediction service, was to lull us into a state of meditation, a state in which the mind was free of all worldly distractions, and was thinking about or of the Divine.

And it worked extremely well, it seemed to me.

We loved the entire exercise, and when the service ended, we left the chapel a little intoxicated by the experience and in an elevated mood.

I don't remember ever not wanting to go to a Mass or a service. I don't remember ever getting bored during one. My mind wandered and my eyes wandered over the many images surrounding me, but the entire experience retained its unique quality, and sent me back out into the world refreshed.

There were other experiences interwoven in this tapestry of beauty and worship, and they also played a part in what faith meant to me.

From the earliest times, my mother read poems to me and my sisters. She had one book of poems which she liked above all, and there were perhaps seven or eight poems she especially loved to read. These weren't religious poems, but she was as regular with this reading as she was with churchgoing; and we learned these poems.

Again, this was a preliterate experience for me. In fact, it was more especially that for me than it was perhaps for others. Because I didn't learn to read from this, as I think perhaps my older sister did. Try as I might, I could never, in later years, read any poem in this book that was not one which my mother had read to me. The audible poem was the only poem that existed for me. I couldn't "hear" the others. And reading did not alter the influence or the feeling invoked in me by these poems. I'll talk more about this later.

Another important element of my childhood was radio.—This was a world that knew nothing of television, but there was a small radio in just about every room in the house, and throughout my childhood the radios were on all day.

I remember lying on the floor listening to the morning soap operas, *Our Gal Sunday* and *The Guiding Light.* Sometimes we listened to Arthur Godfrey in the morning though I can't remember anything he said. At noon we listened to *Ma Perkins,* and then came the parade of afternoon soaps which were a half hour instead of fifteen minutes and inherently much more dramatic. My favorites were *Young Widow Brown* and *Stella Dallas,* and *Lorenzo Jones and His Wife Belle.* As evening came on, the children's programs began which my older sister loved. I suppose everyone else did too since everyone listened. *Jack Armstrong, the All-American Boy* was maybe the first. *Terry and the Pirates* descended on us at some point, and then the king of all shows, *The Lone Ranger,* came on at six.

Nothing came between anyone in my family and *The Lone Ranger.* We moved on into the nighttime realm of the more dangerous shows, shows I call dangerous because they scared me out of my wits.

The Inner Sanctum so traumatized me that I couldn't listen to it after a certain age. But I was also caught unawares by episodes of *Suspense,* or *The Lux Radio Theatre.* And even *The Big Story* could pretty much drive me right out of my head.

What all these shows shared, of course, was that they were narratives being conveyed to us by voices—stories being enacted and told without visual images and certainly without any experience of printed words.

I entered into complete little worlds with these radio shows and emerged from them to enter into more worlds as the day and the night went on.

Weekends brought the big entertainment programs like *Burns and Allen,* or *The Bob Hope Show,* or *The Jack Benny Program,* and though these were amusing and everybody gathered for them, they didn't have the narrative pull of the "story" shows, and the story shows shaped my idea of what a story was, and how important it was.

Either that happened or I simply responded to stories more than anything else.

There was certainly music pouring out of the radio, and it was invariably melodic and gentle. Songs like "Lavender Blue (Dilly Dilly)" or "You're Like a Plaintive Melody, That Never Lets Me Be" were being sung by substantial voices. And I loved all this, but the stories were the key experience for me. When I could lock on to the events of a story, I was happy, or scared, depending on what those elements were.

During these years, we also went to the movies at a small

neighborhood theater on Baronne Street two blocks away. Other than the church, no other place is as vivid to me in retrospect as the Grenada Theater.

Yet the earliest films I recall, I saw downtown in spectacular movie palaces that were fantasies in themselves with great carpeted staircases, huge balconies, and even marble statues in the lobby and on the mezzanine floor.

The first film I recall seeing was *Hamlet.* We were in the balcony, my mother and my sister and I, and my mother was explaining to me what was happening as Hamlet's father was poisoned by his brother. The Ghost was talking. The film was in black-and-white and the images of the murder were fuzzy because it was something the Ghost was describing. The only other scene I recall from this movie was the scene of Ophelia floating away in her madness on a raft of flowers in a stream. It puzzled me very much that she didn't wake up when she fell into the water. I recall arguing about this. It seemed absurd that she simply slipped into the water, speaking soft words and gazing at the sky, and drowned.

Other early movies included *Casablanca,* of which I recall only the final scene between Ingrid Bergman and Humphrey Bogart as they talked beside the plane. I thought it was a dull film. I'd seen, though I don't remember it, a film about the Marx Brothers in Casablanca and I was disappointed that they weren't in this Casablanca film as well. The other notable scene I recall is from *Caesar and Cleopatra,* in which Cleopatra had herself smuggled on board Caesar's ship, wrapped in a rug. That was a fascinating scene to behold:

Vivien Leigh, the gorgeous Cleopatra with her long black hair and curling arm bracelets, coming out of that rug to the amazement of Claude Rains.

It's no accident that I remembered these scenes all my life. It's no accident that I remember listening to the radio so vividly, that I can recall names and even bits of stories from the radio.

Again, all of this was knowledge coming to me audibly and not shaped by printed words. The motion pictures were immense and vital like the church and did not involve the printed word.

And in this preliterate world in which my interests and tendencies and faith were formed, there was a profound connection between narrative, art, music, and faith.

It never occurred to me or anyone I knew that the radio shows were profane, for example, and the church was sacred. The radio shows and the worlds they revealed were as much a part of life as church. Same with films. My mother loved movies, and she told us stories that she had learned from movies. She described movies to us which we all thought would never come to the theaters of our time again. So anything one learned from the radio, from film, from museums, from church—all of it was a rich and wondrous stream in which one could thrive.

The radio brought us not only shows but broadcasts of the Rosary being recited, every evening for fifteen minutes. The Sunday Mass was broadcast over the radio too. My grandmother, long unable to go to church because of her broken hip and her built-up shoe, listened to the Mass in the dining room as she said her Rosary and read *Our Sunday Visitor,* a Catholic newspaper, all at the same time.

When I went to school and began to read, I lost an immense world of image, color, and intricate connections, but undoubtedly I retained more than I lost.

I gained in school a poor understanding of things through written text. School was when excruciating boredom and anger and frustration really began for me. The mystery and calm of the early years were destroyed by school. School was torture. School was like being in jail. It was captivity and torment and failure.

But what remained forever, what continued, was the sense of God and His Presence, of His embracing awareness of us and all we said and did and wanted and failed to do, and of His love. School couldn't destroy that faith. And alongside it, I retained the sense that the world was an interesting creative place, especially if one could get out of school.

Let me emphasize this again: Christian faith was in no way opposed to the world in which I grew up. One didn't leave the world to go to church. Church was simply the most interesting place in the world that I knew. The fact that the school was Catholic and the school taught about God didn't come between me and God. Nothing could do that when I was a child. I simply thought the school was a boring and miserable place. And I think I was right.

3

Be relieved. I don't intend to describe eleven years of Catholic school in the same detail as I've described the world before school. I hated it too much to describe it here. It's much easier to try to draw useful conclusions from what happened than to relive it and wind up in a padded cell.

Before I go on to deal with school in any way, I'd like to talk a little more about my mother. And also I need to talk about my father and my older sister.

If I hadn't known my mother was the primary source of my education when I was little, I certainly knew after a few years of staring out of the window in school.

My mother's whole presentation of the world is what I took away from the first fourteen years of my life.

As I mentioned earlier, she'd read poems to us from before I could recall. My sister, Alice, and I would snuggle up with her on her bed in the smallest and coziest bedroom in the house. The book was called *Two Hundred Best Poems for Boys and Girls* compiled by Marjorie Barrows. It was a small hardcover with a drawing of three timeless little children against a black flowered backdrop.

The poems were illustrated with small silhouettes by Janet Laura Scott and Paula Rees Good. The publisher was the Whitman Publishing Company, in Racine, Wisconsin.

This was the only book from which my mother read to us in the first years. "Song at Dusk" by Nancy Byrd Turner set the tone of my entire life.

> *The flowers nod, the shadows creep,*
> *A star comes over the hill;*
> *The youngest lamb has gone to sleep,*
> *The smallest bird is still.*
> *The world is full of drowsy things,*
> *And sweet with candlelight;*
> *The nests are full of folded wings—*
> *Goodnight, goodnight, goodnight.*

Other poems in the book were filled with pirates, dragons, fairies, and general mystery and magic. My older sister, Alice, liked the more action-packed poems, but I think we agreed on "The Tale of Custard the Dragon" by Ogden Nash.

> *Belinda lived in a little white house,*
> *With a little black kitten and a little gray mouse,*
> *And a little yellow dog and a little red wagon,*
> *And a realio, trulio, little pet dragon.*

The poem goes on for over twelve stanzas, and the gist is that Custard the dragon was a coward who nevertheless proved to be the only brave one in the house when a pirate broke in and threatened them all.

Belinda paled, and she cried, Help! Help!
But Mustard fled with a terrified yelp,
Ink trickled down to the bottom of the household,
And little mouse Blink strategically mouseholed.

But up jumped Custard, snorting like an engine,
Clashed his tail like irons in a dungeon.
With a clatter and a clank and a jangling squirm
He went at the pirate like a robin at a worm.

The reason I've copied out here so many stanzas of this poem is because I think it was significant that we, as little children, were acquainted with this kind of rhythm and vocabulary. Other poems in the book make a similar demand on the mind, and offer a similar musical delight.

Probably nothing I ever wrote as a published author did not derive in some way from the sixteen or so poems my mother chose, over and over again, to read to us from this book. The sheer pleasure of the experience was key.

I spent hours, not reading the poems, but looking at the silhouettes on each page and it did seem to me that these tiny pictures, usually no more than intricate borders for the poems, were filled with mystery.

But her poetry reading was the smallest part of my mother's influence. She told us fabulous stories all the time.

Lying on her bed, listening to her, I learned all about life. She loved to recount her own experiences, how she'd gone to California and lived among a family of movie people, ventured out to a town called Trona to work for a while, lived in Little Rock, Arkansas, though Heaven knows why, and how she'd dated this or that interesting young man, and gone to this or that Mardi Gras ball, or dinner at the yacht club, or how her father—dead in 1917—had been a powerful longshoreman who could carry huge sacks on his shoulders, dazzling other weaker men. She discoursed at length on other people, their psychology, what they were like, and she loved above all perhaps to tell us the plots of movies. *Ben-Hur* she had loved and also *The Count of Monte Cristo,* starring Robert Donat, and there were numerous other films which she sought to make real for us, which we might never see.

Nobody then dreamed of the archival world in which we now live in 2008, a world in which almost any film or book can be retrieved within a matter of hours. Films could be lost in time in those years. Indeed they could be lost forever.

And when precious films returned to the art house theaters for a special run, our mother made sure that we saw them. *The Red Shoes* directed by Michael Powell with Moira Shearer was perhaps the greatest masterpiece to which she exposed us. But she also took me to see Alfred Hitchcock's *Rebecca* with Laurence Olivier and Joan Fontaine. Another film which she took us to see was *A Song to Remember* starring Cornel Wilde as Frédéric Chopin, and Merle Oberon as George Sand, his lover. I was so taken by this film, so taken by the emotions of the young Chopin, when he clutched a handful of Polish earth and swore to remember it, that I wanted nothing more than to have such meaning in my own life, something that precious to me, something to which I could give my whole soul.

In later years we went back to that same art house theater for other extraordinary films, like *The Tales of Hoffmann* or a film of the opera *Aïda* or delightful British comedies about Chesterton's Father Brown and his jewel thief friend Flambeau. This was my mother's doing, this film going, this believing in film as an art form, and seeing it as a door to inspiration and imaginary worlds.

Over and over again, my mother said, "I want to rear four geniuses and four perfectly healthy children." Now, that might frighten a more timid person, but it never frightened me. She told us stories of geniuses of all kinds. She loved describing the vivid social world of Charles Dickens; she recounted to us how the Brontë sisters had written under pen names because they were women and then had taken London by storm as their real selves. She told us the story of the great author George Eliot. She told us about G. K. Chesterton and Hilaire Belloc and Oscar Wilde, whose stories for children we loved. She talked about Madame Curie the great scientist, and she passed on to us bits and pieces of information about her own studies, lectures she'd heard, wise people she'd known, and books she'd read.

I would say she was an irresistible talker, and she did something which now seems to me intensely and distinctively Catholic. She addressed a multitude of questions which had never come up. For example, I remember her explaining to me almost casually why there was no conflict between theories of evolution and the words of the Bible. Genesis tells us God created the world in six days, she would say, but Genesis doesn't tell us how long a day was for God, in God's time. End of conflict.

We were as a family quite interested in evolution, and speculated about it all the time—what had life been like for cavemen? How had they communicated, how had they learned things? My older sister was always finding fossils in the gravel in the backyard. And these were true fossils, some of them, though the stories she told as to what they were had more imagination than scientific preciseness.

There was almost nothing precise about anybody in my childhood.

As the years passed, my older sister brought home fascinating books from the public library, and my mother and my sister read these books together, while I listened to what they said. I remember the whole family becoming enthralled with the life of the ballerina Anna Pavlova. Around that time, we went to see the ballet *Giselle.*

This was an overwhelming sensuous experience—sitting in the fourth or fifth row of an elegant theater (The Civic on Baronne Street downtown, the very same theater that played all the foreign films or artistic films), and watching the exertion and the execution of the dancers at close range.

We also attended a performance of the opera *Carmen* when we were still in grade school; and we started going to the Municipal Auditorium for concerts when I was still in grade school as well.

This was my education, this world of my sister and my mother talking about books, the world in which the radio continued to pour out suspenseful dramas in the evening, and in which classical music was played all the time on the phonograph because we could rent records from the uptown music library, records which we could never have afforded to own.

This was the place where I learned just about anything of importance that I now know.

I cannot imagine my life without my mother or my father or my sister Alice.

My father took us to the library when we were little, and he introduced us to books, yes, and he was a brilliant man. But the core experience for me was not reading these books, because I couldn't. But of discovering that while he was in the Redemptorist Seminary, my father had been a writer, and that in his desk was a treasure trove of poems that he'd written and some short stories as well.

Again, I couldn't really read these things; I couldn't make them my own emotionally by reading. Reading was too difficult. My mind wandered too much. But the idea of my father as a writer was something that blazed like the Burning Bush. My father also wrote a children's novel at this time, called *The Impulsive Imp,* which he read to us chapter by chapter as he developed it. This novel was never published in my childhood, but my father did seek a publisher for it, and even had a friend do illustrations for it, dark paintings, as I recall, which we liked very much.

I, too, wanted to be a writer and struggled with stories

and poems even though I could hardly read. This was the first thing I wanted to do with my whole heart and soul, and the idea that I had to wait to grow up to do it was untenable, and gruesome. Though of course that is what happened.

Let me briefly describe our house. It was a long lower flat in a duplex on the corner of St. Charles Avenue and Philip, and it had two porches on the front, one enclosed by screens, and the other open. French windows opened onto the porches from the living room. Sliding doors divided the living room from my mother's bedroom, and from the main hall. The entrance to the flat was from a side porch, through an alcove that held shelves of books. These books included Chesterton, Dickens, and a row of volumes called the Harvard Classics which my father one day threw away. There were many other interesting books in that alcove. Since I wasn't a reader I never read a single one.

I think my older sister, Alice, whose IQ was on the genius level, probably read every volume. It was said that she read everything in the Children's Library, and that is why she was sneaking upstairs into the Adult Library before she was old enough to do it. That I can believe, and I snuck up to the Adult Library with her.

The house was peculiar. Most of the floors were painted wood and bare. There was a linoleum carpet on the living room floor with a bright flowered pattern, and there were four antique rocking chairs on the four edges of the carpet, and an old studio couch with a pleasant pattern of ribbons and feathers stood against the closed door to my mother's room. Flowered wallpaper covered the walls, and a lovely white marble fireplace and mantel surrounded the small iron gas heater—like almost all the heaters of the house—on its curled legs.

And there was a constant flow in and out on the screened porch, which was considered as private as a room.

My grandmother sat on the screened porch to shell peas in a colander in the evening. I remember stringing peas with her, and shelling them. I remember painting with an easel on this porch later on. Screened porches are all but lost to the world today, but screened porches were wonderful rooms. The soft breezes were always moving through them, yet one felt safe and private from the outside world.

Other things I recall mark this as the end of an era. For example, I recall the iceman rushing up the back steps, with the block of ice on his leather-padded shoulder. I remember the first electric refrigerator that actually kept things cold.

Garbage wagons were pulled by mules, and so was the wagon of the "banana man," invariably black, who sang "Bananas" as he passed.

Laundry was done in tubs in the kitchen, and on a washboard by my grandmother and my mother. I helped lift the twisted sheets out of the wicker basket for my grandmother to hang on the backyard line. There were old clothespins without springs and new clothespins with springs. There were two kinds of soap, Ivory and Octagon.

An old wiggling, shimmying three-legged washing machine with a wringer on it made its way into the house after my grandmother's death. It could waltz out the back door and down the steps if nobody kept watch.

I recall a small portable vacuum cleaner being introduced in later years, but then it was given away to a cousin. The beds had no spreads, only sheets and blankets. They had simple metal headboards. I don't recall anyone ever buying a towel. We had the same towels for fifteen years. I don't recall anyone ever buying a piece of furniture. My mother's wedding china and crystal was broken by us bit by bit as we played with it. We drew on the walls when we wanted to. We cut out paper dolls and pasted them on the walls.

My mother believed in complete creativity; she gave us no chores. She wanted to protect us from chores. My father worked two jobs for months at a stretch, as did most men in those days, and there were long periods when he was seldom there.

Sometime after my grandmother died my mother started to drink in mysterious bouts which involved complete unconsciousness for days. Presumably, she rose in the night, found the liquor she'd stashed away, and drank it until she passed out again.

In between those bouts, she was brilliant and interesting, and for years nothing was said about this "sickness" of hers, except now and then that she was "sick."

By the age of eleven or so, I knew she was dying of this, and I knew that the only way to live was to pretend it wasn't happening. But before I came to this conclusion, I had a breakdown which is worth recording.

I took to my bed for days and refused to get up. I was terrified by visions of the house burning down, of my little sisters trapped in the flames, and my mother, drunk, coughing, unable to get them out.

This must have been summertime when I had this breakdown, because I don't recall anyone saying "Get up and go to school." I remember people sitting on the side of the bed, my mother in particular, and trying to assure me that everything was fine, the house wouldn't burn, and my sisters were fine. Gradually I came back to myself. I stopped shivering in fear. I picked up a book about Raggedy Ann and Andy that was for children smaller than me. I looked at the pictures because it was pleasant, and I healed somehow looking at or reading that book. No words come back to me from it, only the pictures and a feeling of safety, of simplicity, of pleasant things.

My mother's drinking was a great shadow that slowly and steadily darkened our lives.

But our lives went on.

My sister and I went to the library together all the time.

My experience of picking at books was exhilarating, but I remember just as keenly what it felt like to be in the library, to be sitting at a long wooden table in a vast space filled with such tables, sunlight streaming in the tall windows, the air as always warm and rather motionless, and the whole peaceful and safe.

I also recall sitting in "The Stacks," on the green glass floor, and picking through books I couldn't possibly ever understand. I'd read maybe three or four words of some volume like *The Children of Mu,* for example, and despair of ever figuring out the context for what the book was seeking to say.

I never discovered books on art in this library. Maybe there were none. When I was grown up I discovered beautiful art books and went mad for looking at pictures of Rembrandt and Caravaggio and Giotto and Fra Angelico. At this point, I knew none of this by book.

I did know the Delgado Museum of Art in City Park,

however. I'd discovered an art class there on Saturdays, and for years I went to this class, though I never produced anything worth saving by me or anyone else. We were provided with huge sheets of paper, and with plenty of pastels.

Children from all over the city came to this class, though I remember primarily girls. The teachers were gentle and mild mannered and devoted.

But the real experience for me was the museum itself. There I saw large replicas of baroque sculptures, some of which were replicas of Roman and Greek sculptures, and all of which involved Greek gods and goddesses or classical themes, Laocoön and Sons and The Rape of Daphne by Apollo and other such wonderful works. The museum also had some fascinating paintings, largely from the Renaissance on, and I recall interesting lectures on these works.

During the time I went there, an Egyptian exhibit came with a small mummy. That was a landmark event.

City Park itself had a dreamy beauty to it, with meandering lagoons and oaks even bigger than those at Audubon Park uptown. I spent hours as a child, usually with a friend, roaming safely and happily through this park.

I had uncommon freedom as a child. I went just about anywhere that I wanted. And I saw a version of New Orleans that perhaps other children didn't see. I penetrated poor neighborhoods and walked with complete confidence through places where no one would dare to go walking today.

I didn't feel anything could touch me or hurt me. And actually nothing ever did.

The bus trip to the City Park museum took me through

the French Quarter, so, though my family never went there, I experienced it from the bus window as well.

As always I was riveted by the different houses I saw, the iron-lace railings, the elements of Italianate or Greek Revival style, and I was enchanted by color, and New Orleans was and is a city of more colors than one can conceivably name.

Let me repeat: this is the world in which I learned all that I learned. Learning was visual and acoustic but it was not through books. I felt frustrated and shut out of books.

It's important to note that in this world, I did not feel I had any special identity as a child. I did not see my sister as a child, or my younger sisters as children. I moved through this world as a person. We were spoken to by our parents as adults, really, and we called our parents, as they wished it, by their first names.

People were perceived as having distinct personalities and our family was given to labels which could be disruptive and damaging, but essentially it was a world of persons. I wasn't terribly conscious of this, but I know now that I never thought of myself as a child. I will pick up this theme later.

Before I move on in time, let me deal with school.

4

I STARTED THE FIRST GRADE in St. Alphonsus School on St. Andrew Street and Constance in the neighborhood called the Irish Channel. This was a world away from our home on St. Charles Avenue and Philip Street, but only because the five blocks between us took one through the beautiful mansions of the Garden District, from the noise of St. Charles Avenue, to the treeless sun-baked streets of the working-class neighborhood where some of my ancestors had been born. The Irish Channel was at that time still a blue-collar-class neighborhood and the Catholic schools that educated the children were large parish schools.

There were two separate grade schools, as one originally had been for the children of German immigrants and the other was for the children of the Irish, but by my time, immigrant distinctions were largely submerged and how parents made the choice of schools and religious orders I didn't know. I only knew that I was going to St. Alphonsus, staffed by the Sisters of Mercy, and that my two aunts were both Sisters of Mercy, and that this was our school. My mother had gone there, in the very same building, many years before.

The uniforms were simple: any kind of white cotton blouse, and any kind of navy blue skirt. Everyone wore brown string shoes. The children of the parish were entirely too poor to have any fancier uniform than this. Prim little girls had navy blue sweaters and pleated skirts. Poorer children wore what they had. Everybody was supposed to have a blue beanie. If you didn't have a beanie on your head, you weren't supposed to go into church. No woman with an uncovered head ever went into church. And no man went in without taking off his hat.

The boys had nothing to do with our world. They were in their own schools, staffed, it seemed to me, by much harsher and rougher sisters who slapped them often in an endless struggle to make them behave. We caught glimpses of them and their fearsome teachers when we assembled for church. At a distance, they seemed loud and noisy and disruptive, and infinitely more rambunctious than girls.

We were a classroom of forty little girls with a young teacher, Sister Mary Hyacinth, and the first thing I did when I was introduced to this sister, was tell this sister that my name was Anne.

Up until that time I'd been called Howard Allen, which was in fact my name. I had been named after my father, Howard, and after my mother, as her maiden name was

Allen, and each of her daughters carried that name as well. My parents had insisted on this startlingly unusual name for me even when the baptizing priest objected that there was no St. Howard, and insisted that the name Frances be added, as there was a St. Frances indeed. But I never knew as a little girl that I had the name of Frances, any more than I knew that I'd been born on the Feast Day of St. Francis of Assisi, a saint I came to love more than any other saint.

What I did know was that my parents thought the male name of Howard was going to be a great asset to me, and they also believed that I was going to do great things.

I hated it. Children on my block had always objected vigorously to this name. "That's a boy's name." I didn't like the sound of it. If it had been Mark Antonio, or Celestino, I might have loved it. Sidney, Valentino, Louis Philippe, any name of that sort, I might have tolerated. But Howard Allen was the ugliest, most confusing, jarring and burdensome name imaginable, and I parked it at the door. I walked away from it into the name of Anne.

My mother went along with it. If she wants to be called Anne, she said, then call her Anne. Sister Hyacinth was amused. And later on at recess, when I told my sister Alice, who was always called Suzie, that I wanted to be Anne, she started calling me Anne. This was a highly influential moment. If my sister had made war on this name, the war might have been won. But she accepted it with a near eerie wisdom and thenceforth called me Anne until she died. Every now and then over the years, she'd slip and call me Howard Allen but it was never intentional, and probably she wasn't even aware of it, and I didn't mark it either.

But that recess where I encountered her in the alien school yard and she addressed me as Anne was decisive.

As for the building and the yard, they seemed ancient. The highly polished steps in the school building were so old that they were worn concave and the nail heads were slightly raised though still sunk deep in the waxed wood. The stairs had beautifully carved banisters. As for the yard it was vast, sprawling, and plain with nothing much that I recall except a fig tree at one end surrounded by benches, and a chain-link fence along the street. There was an overhang under which we could play during the rain. And through the windows we could peep secretively into the sisters' dining room where they were ranged down a long table, saying their Grace Before Meals with folded hands, or actually eating their meal.

To see a sister eat her meal in those days was something that wasn't supposed to happen. Nuns went everywhere by twos, they did not drive automobiles, and they never ate or drank in public at all. So this peeping in the windows was quick when it happened, and all I recall were shadowy shapes.

Let me take this opportunity to say something about the nuns of this era. I went through four years with the Sisters of Mercy in this building. And later I went through four years with the Sisters of Mercy at Holy Name of Jesus School uptown. All these nuns, except for Sister Hyacinth, were older women, and they worked almost unbelievably hard. Some of them were ancient; all were extremely self-sacrificing with lives completely devoted to teaching; they took vows of poverty, chastity, and obedience. They wore heavy ornate black habits, with extraordinarily stiff white wimples, and negotiated every gesture and task in spite of voluminous deep black sleeves. They lived their whole lives in the convent buildings. If they had vacations I knew nothing about them. And if they possessed anything for themselves I never saw any evidence of it. It was understood by us that they lived as celibate and dedicated religious because their work for God required this, and they were perceived as Brides of Christ in their purity and single-minded devotion. Their names tended to be otherworldly: Sister Annunciata; Sister Bernard; Sister Damien; Sister Francesca; Sister Beatrice; Sister Therese Marie.

Later in high school, I was immeasurably helped and guided by members of the School Sisters of Notre Dame. These were younger women, highly educated, and extremely refined. They were from the North. And I remember them as extraordinarily patient with my eccentricities, rebelliousness, and general determination to be a great person, rather than a good student. These nuns were also extremely kind to my sister Alice, who, though she had a genius IQ, did poorly in school. They even sent her to a state competition in history, in which she placed second. And normally, a student as poor as my sister would never have been given such an opportunity. They saw her abilities and they valued her for them. And when my sister placed high in that competition, she was overjoyed.

I remember particularly Sister Caroline, and the principal, Sister Caroleen.

All nuns of these years were exquisitely dressed. Almost every order had its distinctive soft fine black wool robes and its own particular and elaborate headdress. They were decidedly medieval in appearance, and effortlessly grand.

Even the Little Sisters of the Poor, who dressed somewhat more simply than others, wore beautiful white caps with ruffled edges, and lovely loose-hooded black mantles.

All nuns covered their hair entirely. And usually their necks were covered as well.

I recall them as an ebullient people, intensely interested in their charges and as having great authority. In sum, they educated the Catholics of my generation—male and female— in the highly complex teachings of the Catholic Church, and they taught not only grade school but high school. The Dominican sisters taught college.

There were teaching brothers and teaching priests, most notably the Jesuits, but the nuns staffed the countless parish schools of the country, and to them fell the responsibility for thousands of Catholic minds. When I look back on it, I have only the deepest respect for their remarkable self-discipline and the difficult life that they had chosen, and their full commitment to it. The example they set for me was one of independence and strength, because even though they weren't so friendly to my independence and strength, they were remarkable women themselves.

There are great stories to be written about these nuns— about how their various orders were formed, and how these orders often fought with the male hierarchy of the church to gain the freedom to minister directly to the people, at times when the hierarchy wanted to put these sisters in cloisters and keep them out of the active world.

The brilliant historian Diarmaid McCulloch writes a good deal about this in his huge and comprehensive work, *The Reformation.* And no doubt there are many other books written, and to be written. Recently, the author Kenneth Briggs published a book called *Double Crossed: Uncovering the Catholic Church's Betrayal of American Nuns.* But Mr. Briggs' work covers a period of church history after Vatican II, and a time when I was estranged from the church, and a long way from the period I'm describing here.

As a child, I wasn't aware of the battles the great mother superiors had fought in past centuries; or of the strange tension that existed between powerful nuns and male clergy. I wasn't aware of the tension that had sometimes existed between great female saints and male clergy—except, of course, for the tragic story of Joan of Arc. The interplay of nuns and priests appeared seamless to me in my childhood, a world shared by male and female religious. And one cannot exaggerate the striking power of the nuns of those years.

In this realm in which I'd been brought up, being a nun or a priest was deemed to be much better than being married or being single. It was understood that a dedicated, and celibate, nun or priest could come to understand things mystically that no nonvirginal person could aspire to grasp.

We were privileged to have two aunts that were nuns, and we were keenly aware of it. Sister Mary Immaculate, Aunt Anna Mae, was my father's sister, and she was a nurse. In fact, I believe that she was the superintendent of nurses at Mercy Hospital for many years. We saw her often because she lived all her life in New Orleans, and she died in Mercy Hospital in the 1970s. Only after her death did I hear that she had gone blind when she was a child, and had promised to become a nun if her sight was restored. After the restoration she made good on her promise. She had an especially beautiful smile, this aunt, and that's perhaps why I still connect the basket of flowers with her name.

Our older aunt, Sister Mary Liguori, Aunt Helen, was my grandmother's sister, and the last of thirteen children. Her field was education and she spent most of her life in Bethesda, Maryland. When Aunt Helen came to town, we were bathed, dressed up, and sent to visit her, and I remember being much in awe of her, of her seriousness and her directness. She lived until the 1990s, and died in her sleep, during noon Mass, in the infirmary of Mercy Hospital. That my young son, Christopher, born in 1978, had come to know Aunt Helen, even briefly, was a great joy to me.

As children, we were proud, too, of the fact that my father had received his exceptional education in the Redemptorist Seminary at Kirkwood, Missouri, because he had wanted to become a priest. As far as I know, no one ever criticized my father for his decision not to become a priest, and he was a deeply devoted Catholic all his life. He belonged to an organization called the Holy Name Men, one of many such organizations in the parish, and he went out on Sundays with our uncle Cecil Murphy to visit the elderly and care for the needy of the parish. Over the years, my father told me several different stories as to why he didn't become a priest. One thing is certain: his education by the Redemptorist Fathers changed the entire course of his life. He was one of nine children who had grown up in one half of a double house one block from the river and its noisy railroad tracks. And he came home from the seminary a well-spoken, well-educated man.

Both priests and nuns were the guardian angels of my Catholic childhood. And they were, in the main, gentle with the girls, as I've indicated, though we did now and then glimpse them being quite ferocious with the boys. I can't look back on those times without feeling a special reverence for those in religious life; and happily, I remember how beautifully visible they were in the Catholic city of New Orleans, nuns in pairs, riding free on the streetcars and buses, and the priests often wearing their full-length black cassocks, with large rosaries hanging from their broad leather belts.

I felt a special kinship for the Redemptorist Fathers. They had educated my father. And they were our priests. They were passionate in their sermons, and frequently their sermons were events. I remember being riveted by the description of how the Romans had martyred a young male saint. And I recall the passionate anti-Communist words spoken from the pulpit. I don't know how many priests there were in our parish, except there were a great number and they were always busy, coming and going from the rectory on Constance Street, saying Masses in two giant churches and in one nearby chapel, and hearing Confessions from an enormous body of parishioners on Friday nights. I remember names like Father McCarthy, Father O'Connoll, Father Flynn, Father Greenberg, Father Steffens, Father Baudry, Father Dillenbeck, Father Toups. I don't remember anyone ever calling a priest by his first name in those days. And I never heard the slightest word of scandal regarding these men. In fact, it's almost impossible to believe there was any scandal. And perhaps in those days, in that parish, there was not.

Let me return now to that first school building.

There were two lush and lovely gardens attached to this property, one on either side of the main building, and we did often pass through one of these gardens to go into the music room. The other was the nuns' garden, and that was a matter for peeping again.

I have one special and radiant memory connected to the garden by the music room. We were passing there one day, perhaps to go to sing in preparation for a school pageant, when we came upon a group of older girls who were gathered there because they were making a "Retreat."

Now a Retreat is a period of a few days during which one remains totally silent, and prays and listens to sermons on religious matters; there were closed Retreats at Retreat Houses to which Catholics went where they remained under strict rules of silence both day and night. And there were open Retreats which we made at some point during the school year.

And as we came into this garden, one of the girls, my cousin Kitty Belle Murphy, looked up and smiled at me and greeted me cheerfully and kindly by my old name. "Well, how do you do, Howard Allen?" she said with a lovely generosity that was characteristic of her every time I ever spoke to her.

I remember being startled, not by the old name, but by the friendliness with which she greeted me, that she didn't mind people knowing I was her cousin. I already had a profound sense by then that I was a rather disreputable or questionable person. And Kitty Belle Murphy was perfect in every respect.

She was the youngest girl in a family of eight which was a model Christian family, and her mother, our aunt Lillian, was one of the most beloved people in our world. Uncle Cecil Murphy, the father of the eight children, was the perfect model of a Catholic man. Kitty had a great glowing generosity of spirit very like her mother, and she remains in this memory of mine nestled among the flowers and near to the Grotto of the Virgin, a large stone edifice, in which the Blessed Mother stood with arms out, appearing to the kneeling figure of St. Bernadette. No Catholic school existed in those days that didn't have a grotto, with the Virgin and St. Bernadette. We all knew the Virgin had appeared to St. Bernadette in Lourdes, France, and that there was a great miraculous shrine there where people were constantly healed by the powerful waters that had sprung from the earth at the command of the Virgin to Bernadette.

Kitty was a saint for me as certainly as was Bernadette. Indeed, Kitty had a saintly and lovely sister named Bernadette, and she too was a shining light in my childhood, and my years of growing up. After my mother's death, the Murphy girls were like my elder sisters, and they helped me with many of the small problems that a teenage girl confronts. The steady light cast by the whole Murphy family, in their old-fashioned Catholic perfection, has illuminated my life up to the present time. In a real way, they deserve their own book, the Murphy family. Seven of the eight children are living, and they and their grandchildren and great-grandchildren are an endangered species indeed.

Back to the first-grade classroom:

What we learned in this school immediately was to write in a perfect Palmer-style hand. We learned this from books of Palmer script, making pages of *a*'s and then *b*'s and moving on through the alphabet. We never learned to print.

We learned to read from an insipid reader filled with fantastical pictures of Dick and Jane and Father and Mother who lived in a fantastical house with a monkey. We knew these were supposed to be ordinary people. But they looked to us like millionaires in a world of luxury that had nothing to do with our own.

They weren't related to the kinds of houses in which we lived, and they had nothing to do with the great mansions of the Garden District. I had some vague sense that they were "American" and "normal." It was a bore. "See Dick run." I learned it but I didn't learn how to sink into a book or embrace it. And these readers probably had nothing to do with the failure either way.

We also learned the catechism, which was far more interesting to read, and this was my first formal instruction in religion that had to do with printed words.

My difficulties with reading prevented me from ever absorbing it as written material. I remember it as a series of rhythmic recitations:

Who made us? God made us.

Why did God make us? God made us to show forth His goodness and to share with us His everlasting happiness in Heaven.

Who is God? God is the Supreme Being.

We learned to recite this out loud, and though we did eventually learn to copy the questions and answers in pencil or ink, it was the rhythm that lodged in my mind.

Now compare the above to "See Dick run." Which is more interesting? Religion as the catechism taught it was infinitely more interesting. Think about the lovely sound of the word "everlasting." Reading lines like "See Dick run" was a bit like playing scales, I suppose. Whatever the case, the readers meant nothing until they started to have real stories in them in the fifth grade. The catechism shaped the learning that sparked my attention and my imagination, and began to fill up my head.

Our classrooms were large with huge windows that were open to the breezes that kept us cool even in periods of stifling heat which people in our air-conditioned world would not have borne. There were pictures of the saints in these classrooms, and there were statues, but I don't remember any of them. I think every room had a crucifix. I think every room might have had a picture of Pope Pius XII. It saddens me that I can't remember these details, and that the building, destroyed by Hurricane Betsy, in the sixties, is long gone.

The students in the school were white. These were the days of segregation and I did not ever hear of a school in our neighborhood for "colored" Catholics, and as far as I know there was none. Where these children were educated, I have no idea.

There were in fact many educated black people in New Orleans, and they did have schools, but they were not part of our world. I learned about them much later, when I began to roam the city, and even then the sight of them, these solid middle-class black people, was a bit of a shock.

The people of this time were vigorously racist. Though my parents were not, they accepted segregation as something that had to exist. They actively taught us not to be racist. But they were not social activists. I was not acutely aware of these issues at six years of age. But I lived in a white world of women and little girls. My father, a beloved uncle, and the priests were the only men.

Soon after I entered first grade, we began to prepare for our First Confession and our First Communion, and I think, though I'm not sure, that we went to daily Mass in the nearby church of St. Alphonsus, which was, and is, one of the most engulfingly beautiful places I've ever been.

At this point in my life, this was surely the largest structure I'd ever seen, except perhaps for the church of the Holy Name uptown, and St. Alphonsus was a much more intricately and opulently decorated church. The stained-glass windows are a marvel in themselves. I remember long periods in the pews, when I would study these windows, and the one which has proved unforgettable is the window in which the Boy Jesus appears before the Elders in the Temple, and proves to be admirable and wise. These were romantic and robust depictions, just like the other images in the church, which included vibrant and elaborate murals on the ceiling— of Jesus ascending into Heaven above the assembled Apostles—and numerous other portraits of saints.

A giant mural or fresco stood above the main altar of the church, and the altar was extremely impressive as were the four side altars which this church contained. Our Mother of Perpetual Help had her own special altar to the right of the main altar, and on the far left, on the other side of the church, was the altar of St. Joseph. Two other altars stood against the side walls of the church. And there were times, early in the morning, when Mass was being said on all five altars, because the parish had a large staff of priests, and all priests in those days had to celebrate Mass each day at least once.

Coming to this church for 5:30 a.m. Mass with my mother was an experience, after which we had soft drinks—an unusual treat—at a little restaurant on St. Charles Avenue before going home.

To the right of the altar, and down farther into the body of the church, there was a giant crucifix hung against one of the many Corinthian columns that made up the church. Our Lord on the cross looked resigned with His eyes closed. At His feet stood His sorrowful Mother, whom we sometimes called the Mater Dolorosa, or simply Our Lady of Sorrows. And I liked to talk to Our Lord on this cross.

Throughout my early years, I witnessed sumptuous Masses and services in this church.

Midnight Mass that first year for me involved a procession in which we first-grade girls were angels with heavy wings strapped to our backs, and we moved out of the sanctuary, and down the center aisle, two by two, over what I recall as a carpet of flower petals.

Benediction in this church, that is, the adoration of the Blessed Sacrament, was a splendid affair, and I recall once the priest moving down the center aisle and up another, with a canopy carried over him and the monstrance with which he blessed all those he passed.

To attend the Stations of the Cross in this church was profoundly inspiring, with the priest and two altar boys moving from Station to Station, announcing the name of the Station—for example, the first, "Jesus Is Condemned to Death," or the Sixth Station, "Veronica Wipes the Face of Jesus," or the Eleventh Station, "Jesus Is Nailed to the Cross"—and then reciting the prayer for that particular moment on Jesus' journey to the tomb.

The prayers being recited by the priest had been written by St. Alphonsus Liguori, the patron saint of our parish and our church and the saint who founded the Order of the Redemptorist Fathers who staffed our parish and all its schools and its two churches and its chapel in the Garden District.

After the recitation of the prayer for the Station, we sang a verse of a long continuous sad and tender hymn. At the First Station, the verse went:

> *At the Cross her station keeping,*
> *Stood the mournful Mother weeping,*
> *Close to Jesus to the last.*

After the Fourteenth Station, "Jesus Is Placed in the Sepulcher," the concluding verse ran:

> *Virgin of all Virgins best*
> *Listen to my fond request,*
> *Let me share thy grief divine.*

This was quite an experience even for me in my youngest years—intense, and deliberately sorrowful and purposeful and satisfying as rich food or drink.

But to return to the momentous events of first grade, learning to make one's First Confession was keenly important and then First Communion was a bit like a little wedding, as we girls wore the most stunningly beautiful white dresses that our parents could find, and wreaths of white flowers in our specially curled hair. We also wore rouge and lipstick for this.

Later, at age twelve, Confirmation, which I "made" in Holy Name of Jesus Church, near Loyola University, was another little wedding, on an even grander scale. Our dresses were fancier and more expensive, and this time we wore not only the white wreaths of flowers, but exquisite veils thrown back over the wreaths to form beautiful layers of white netting trimmed in a thorn stitch of white silk.

These were the big sacraments of being Catholic. And they were high points of Catholic life for everyone involved.

The First Confession I recall with some pain. This came before First Communion, and I was perhaps six years old.

We were taught how to examine our consciences and determine what sins we had committed; and we were told that we had to be extremely thorough, and confess every single sin that we could recall. To deliberately leave out a sin was a terrible sin, a sin of sacrilege that would invalidate the Confession and of course leave one in a state of sin which was devoutly to be avoided at all costs. When the priest gave us absolution, our sins would be forgiven, absolutely completely wiped away. The penance given by the priest would be a matter of Hail Marys or Our Fathers. I never remember it being more than that during the entire time I was growing up.

Now, I was six years old at this time, as I said, which meant, strictly speaking, I had not reached the Age of Reason. So I wasn't really qualified to commit a sin. However, I was going to be seven soon enough, and I was painfully conscious of what that meant. At the age of seven I could commit a mortal sin and go to Hell forever for it. And so the Confession went forward, and the Confession was of the utmost importance.

We also learned at that time that there were two kinds of sins, mortal sins and venial sins, and this was a lesson that has stayed with me, in one form or another, all my life. I don't think I've ever stopped thinking of sin in terms of two kinds of sins.

A mortal sin was of course the worst. If one died with a mortal sin on one's conscience, one went to Hell. I vaguely recall the question in the catechism, "What three things are necessary to make a sin mortal?" I've been unable to find a reprint of the catechism that has the answer I can only partially reproduce. It went something like "The matter must be grievously wrong, the sinner must know that it is grievously wrong, and the sinner must have full intent to commit the sin." There's a great deal to ponder in this answer. But let me move on to the description of venial sin which I can take now from a reprint of the 1933 edition of the *Baltimore Catechism*:

Venial sin is a slight offence against the law of God in matters of less importance; or in matters of great importance it is an offence committed without sufficient reflection or full consent of the will.

Again, there's a lot to ponder here, because the description is both detailed and comprehensive and describes human actions on a multitude of levels and from different points of view.

As a little child, I found nothing confusing in any of this. It seemed logical and of a piece with the images in the church, the complex and ever unfolding story of Jesus' life on earth, and the entire picture of God in Heaven and the faithful down here struggling to do His will.

I remember standing in the back of the church with other little girls waiting nervously for this first Confession. The confessional box was a tall tri-part affair made of black wood. The priest sat in the center compartment, behind a little black wooden gate, and with a green curtain hanging above it, and those who wanted to confess entered to kneel in compartments on either side. The priest alternated between sides, opening a screen to hear the Confession of the kneeling person whom the priest could hardly see. To those of us going to Confession, the priest was a profile and a voice.

I was afraid I'd forget something; I went back over and over my sins. But I don't recall now what they were. I suspect they focused on the Fourth Commandment: "Honor thy father and thy mother." It did seem this was the most important challenge facing me at that point. I don't recall the Confession itself. I recall others over the years, as I went to Confession every week after that right up through the age of seventeen.

But that first one in particular I don't recall. I recall rather the shadowy aisle of the church and the immensity of the confessional, and the utter seriousness of this confrontation with the reality of sin.

On the day of my First Communion, the only thing I really cared about was my white dress, my paper wreath of white flowers, and those I'd visit afterwards as the special little girl who'd just made her First Communion.

Someone at some point told us that Napoléon Bonaparte had once said that the happiest day of his life was that of his First Communion. I felt dreadfully inadequate after hearing that. There was no doubt in my mind that I lacked that kind of depth. And years later when I discovered Napoléon had been about twelve when he made his First Communion, I was distinctly relieved. After all, I'd been only six.

Now this is the memory I hold sacred from that day.

After the ceremony I was taken to old Mercy Hospital on the riverfront to visit the nuns. My aunt Anna Mae of the beautiful name was there, no doubt, though I don't recall her. I do remember being in the garden with the sisters, another one of those lovely places with which my childhood is filled.

I suppose you couldn't have a Catholic institution without a lush and beautiful garden. You couldn't have a hospital, an old folks' home, a boarding school or a grammar school without that mysterious place set apart for blossoms, within brick walls.

And I recall an ancient nun, a kitchen sister, all in white with an apron, coming into the hospital garden and telling me with a radiant face that this was a wonderful day because my soul was so pure. She was thin, almost wraithlike, and she made me think of driftwood; but the look of joy on her face and the enthusiasm with which she said these words were breathtaking to me. She seemed utterly and completely sincere and in the presence of a magnificent concept that went beyond anyone or anything present.

She is the memory of my First Communion, and I never knew her name—a woman who came out of the kitchen in her white apron to tell me gently and with immense conviction what it meant that my immortal soul was pure.

After First Communion I went all the time to Mass and Communion, and in those days this involved a total fast from midnight. One could not drink a drop of water. One could eat not a crumb. But it didn't matter. This was part of the way things were, and Mass was the way to begin every single day.

Even in summer, when we did not have the sisters to herd us into the church, my mother roused us. "He's three blocks away," she would say. "He's on that altar. Now get up and go." She'd have breakfast ready when we came home.

By second grade, we were reading "Bible history," and this was our beginning of understanding the Bible as a collection of tales. It is true that Catholics of this period did not learn the Bible. And I don't ever recall seeing a Bible in our house. We weren't forbidden to study it; we simply didn't do it. The Gospel on Sunday was a reading by the priest from the New

Testament; the Epistle on Sunday was a reading from the letters of St. Paul. I don't think I ever really understood who St. Paul really was, except that he had written the Epistles read to us on Sunday, but why or when I did not know.

I never understood the Epistles. They struck me as vague and abstract.

Our study of "Bible history" told us the tales of both Old and New Testaments, which we learned from little books with delicate pen illustrations in which the biblical figures were appealingly drawn.

Recently I've examined several editions of the *Illustrated Bible History* by Dr. I. Schuster. And I'm fairly certain we used a version of this material, though precisely which edition I don't know. What strikes me as I look at the books now is that the stories of the Bible are detached from the voice or name of any particular book of the Bible, and though much biblical language is used, there are also sections of teaching which do not come directly from Scripture. For example, right after the words of God condemning Adam—"for dust thou art, and into dust thou shalt return"—there comes a paragraph which reads "How great is the mercy of God, that He promised a Redeemer to our sinful parents." This is not in the Bible as far as I know.

After the story of Cain slaying his brother Abel, there comes this line: "The innocent Abel slain by his envious brother is a figure of Christ."

The point here is this: I grew up on these little Bible histories, reading more and more with each passing grade from school, and though they gave me an immersion in biblical literature, I did not come out of it really knowing Scripture itself.

The emphasis here is on incident and not on the biblical voice.

When we came to the life of Jesus in our Bible histories, we moved into a harmonized version of Jesus' life, with no specific reference to an Evangelist as the source of the details we read. Though the words of Christ appeared in these stories, we did not have the stylistic flavor of the individual Gospel. Certainly there was no sense that the Gospels contradicted one another or challenged one another because there was no sense of the individual Gospels.

I recall loving this material and reading it with interest, though again I can hardly call it reading. I took the information from the page, but I never sank into the prose and rode along with it into another realm.

Later on in school, and in the library, I did go through many types of books. Those that held my interest were principally Greek myths and lives of the saints.

I discovered the wondrous world of Greek myths at the public library, and I read the lives of the saints in the library at school. I could follow this type of material because of action and incident, and I felt I was gaining information from it which I could apply directly to my own life. It had little to do with the style of the writing or with any imaginary world created by a particular author's prose.

Books that demanded that type of surrender were over my head.

I also read in the library books about prehistoric times and about ancient Egypt and ancient Greece. Pictures in these books had a powerful effect, and the topics were frequently discussed at length in our house. I fell in love with the lore and art of ancient Egypt. The realm of Greek mythology remained an obsession with me all my life.

And I recall vividly studying small marble Greek statues of gods and goddesses that decorated the lobby and mezzanine of the beautiful Saenger Theatre downtown. These statues were elaborate and true to baroque models, something I couldn't know, but could only sense. The theater had huge Greek statues way up at the tops of its walls, and I loved to gaze up at these statues at times when the movies were not so interesting. The ceiling of the Saenger Theatre was the dark blue night sky, covered with stars.

Greek mythology, stories of the gods, stories of the ancient Egyptians, all this intrigued me and excited me, but precious little discussion of any of this occurred in the classroom.

No one ever suggested that there was any tension between studying classical times or ancient times, or prehistoric times and being a believing Catholic. This was all legitimate and profitable knowledge, and conversation at home involved it all.

As for the lives of the saints, I was able to pick away at the stories, especially those written for children. By the sixth and seventh grades, I read these almost exclusively, never attempting any fiction written for children, which seemed to me a waste of time. My curiosity about history was building. I remember being swept up in a life of Leonardo da Vinci to the point where I fell in love with him. I pored over a lurid history of the Roman emperors and their debaucheries which gave me nightmares.

It's important here to note that there were saints of all

kinds for study, and that there were as many female saints as male saints.

In fact, I never associated gender with a saint.

St. Rose of Lima with her spectacular penances and supernatural abilities was as interesting as St. Ignatius Loyola who had founded the Jesuits; after all, St. Rose of Lima could toss roses in the air which formed a floating cross. St. Martin de Porres, who could be in two places at one time (the gift of bilocation), was as fascinating as St. Teresa of Avila who founded the Discalced Carmelites and wrote her own autobiography, a book with which I struggled pretty much in vain. St. Cecilia, the patron saint of musicians, was fabulously interesting, not only because she was beautifully pictured with an organ or a harp, but because she had been a valiant martyr, and her persecutors had tried, without success, to suffocate her in her lavish Roman bath. Sometimes the sufferings of the saints were too much for me. I shuddered when I read about St. Lawrence being roasted alive. I questioned my own courage in the face of his example. I preferred to read the colorful adventures of saints like Francis of Assisi who accomplished great things without the necessity of a bloody death.

I also chipped away, during those years, at *The Imitation of Christ* by Thomas à Kempis, and at *The Spiritual Exercises of St. Ignatius* but gained very little, and went back to the narrative adventures of heroism that never failed to carry me along.

There was St. Alphonsus, who had founded the Redemptorist Fathers of our parish. And St. Elizabeth of Hungary, who had given so much to the poor. There was St. Lucy, whose eyes had been put out during her martyrdom. And St. Agnes, who had died a martyr as well. There were saints from all periods of church history, and this included our own times. St. Thérèse, The Little Flower, had lived only a short time ago. And most recently, St. Maria Goretti, a lovely young Italian girl, had died rather than give up her chastity to an attacker, and had been canonized by Pope Pius XII.

We all wanted to be like Maria Goretti. We would have died rather than give up our chastity, of course.

But I hungered for something beyond martyrdom—the greatness of St. Francis of Assisi, leaving his rich father, to found the Franciscan Order and reform the entire church. I hungered for a spectacular life of extraordinary triumphs, and I don't think I understood anything really about obedience or humility in terms of this sort of life. The idea for me was to be exceptional, to be great.

All these saints had their emblems or tokens, and many of their statues filled our churches. St. Rita, a tall dark-clad nun, always had the wound in her forehead, through which she suffered willingly for Christ. I remember standing in front of her statue in the back of St. Alphonsus Church and praying to her in the hopes that she would help me to love suffering, which in fact I intensely disliked.

St. Catherine, the martyr, was always pictured with a wheel. St. Lucy, her eyes miraculously restored, held the first pair on a plate. We visited her statue in St. John the Baptist Church and prayed to her there. St. Teresa of Avila held a feather quill because she was, on account of her writings, a Doctor of the Church. St. Agnes, in the small holy pictures we treasured, always had her lamb beside her. And St. Louis of France, perhaps my favorite at one time, was pictured with his golden crown, as he had been the king of France.

On the corner of Josephine Street and Constance Street, one-half block from St. Alphonsus Church and right across the street from St. Mary's Church, stood the "holy stores," or two shops that sold statues, rosaries, and holy pictures. And I loved collecting these holy pictures of the saints.

When I was about twelve, I persuaded my father to clean up a little unused room on our back porch, and to paint it so that it would become an oratory for me, like the oratory used by St. Rose of Lima in her family garden in Peru.

My father did a wonderful job. I remember he painted the walls a beautiful shade of gray. And I put up lovely gilded holy pictures all around the walls of this little room. I spent time in it praying. I was trying to be a saint.

In school, Bible history at some point gave way to church history, and this held my interest because of the high level of incident and the narrative flow.

I lost the real thread of what was happening, but I recall spectacular events like the Greek Schism when Eastern Catholics split off from Roman Catholics, and also the time of the Babylonian Captivity when the pope did not reside at Rome; there came a troubled time when there were three men claiming to be popes. At some point, St. Catherine of Siena, one of the greatest saints ever, went to the true pope and persuaded him to return to Rome where the true pope should always live. I was overwhelmed by the life of St. Catherine of Siena. In her zeal to serve the Lord, after nursing lepers, she took the washbasin she'd been using for this and drank the water. I wanted the courage to do something as great.

With regard to the Bible, I continued to hear it in the readings at Mass, and the words were deeply poetic and impressive. Surely I became acquainted that way with many incidents in the life of Christ, but again, I had no sense of the overall flow.

Whatever the case, I came out of Catholic school knowing all the important people and incidents of the Bible, without a sense of its distinctiveness, its idiosyncrasies, or its poetic qualities. I had little sense at all of the Bible's voice.

And I came out with a strong sense of the history of the church—at least up to the Reformation—and of the lives of the saints. As for the Reformation, it was described to us in wholly negative terms. Martin Luther, we were taught, had been a deeply flawed human being. Horrified by the corruption he saw in Rome, he had recoiled from the whole church. And because he himself could not be perfect according to the rules of the faith, he had rebelled against them, something which we in our humility must never do.

Protestant religions were not true religions, and they differed from us in one striking and essential way. Protestants didn't believe in good works, we were told, and we knew that good works were essential. "Faith without good works is dead." That was our motto, and that was the motto of every Catholic hospital or sanitarium or Catholic school.

But all this was theoretical to me, as I knew no Protestants. And I couldn't imagine people who didn't believe in good works. I couldn't grasp what such a Christian life could possibly mean. The whole world around me was Catholic. The city of New Orleans as I knew it was divided into church parishes and each one had its church and school. There was no area where there was no Catholic parish. I lived on a Catholic map.

An extremely important aspect of all my schooling was this: we lived and breathed our religion and our religion was interesting, and vast, and immensely satisfying, and we had an unshakable sense of the "goodness" of Catholic education, and we were also aware of something else. There was no better all-around education to be had in other schools. We were learning science and arithmetic and history and geography just as any child in public school would be learning them, and we had no sense of being insulated from anything that those children might be learning. We felt we were getting a thorough and practical education and more.

Our teachers never spoke of any conflict between religion and science. We were never taught that there were theories or ideas about science or social science that we couldn't believe. In sum, there was nothing defensive or especially protective about our Catholic education. We weren't being kept away from anything. We were being given everything and more. Indeed, we were to leave the schools well equipped for the world on all levels, but we would take with us a stronger sense of our religion than other people might have.

We were convinced as well that the discipline of our schools was an outstanding feature.

At those times when the whole school attended a motion picture downtown, or went to the Municipal Auditorium for a concert, we were proud of the order and quiet that we reflected as a body of students, compared to the unruly and noisy crowds of public school students taking their places with a lot of shouting and talking and moving around.

Around the freshman year of high school, I began to actually read. The first novel that I recall truly enjoying and loving for its language as well as its incident was *Great Expectations* by Charles Dickens which was in our textbook. We read it week by week. The other novel I discovered in the school library. It was Charlotte Brontë's *Jane Eyre.*

Surrendering to the world created by the written word was not only wholly new to me but difficult, and I think it took me a year to consume these two books. It might have taken two years. I can still remember the classroom in which we were reading Dickens. And I can remember the table in the school library where I read chapter after chapter of *Jane Eyre.*

It's worth noting here that I identified strongly with Pip, the hero of Dickens' novel, and also with Jane in Brontë's novel.

In fact, all during these years I identified as easily with male figures as with female figures, and took no note of any particular distinction having to do with being male or female.

The "he" used in books to refer to humanity was inclusive for me. It did not occur to me that statements involving "man" or "humankind" or "us" in the catechism did not include me. As for the saints, let me repeat, there were saints of both sexes, and the gender of a saint seemed to be the least important characteristic of a saint. True, there was a passive St. Clare connected with the active St. Francis. But within convents, there were powerful mystics like St. Margaret Mary, whose visions of the Sacred Heart of Jesus transformed the world. Or so it seemed.

None of the books I read, including these magnificent novels, made me a true reader. For the first time, I did imbibe style with Dickens and Brontë, and I loved it. But it was slow go.

I continued to listen for knowledge and continued to hang on the words of those who said interesting things. I continued to look forward to the moments in class when the teacher told a story, or rambled on about personal experience, or gave her opinions, and though I'd accumulated the names of many authors, I felt unable to penetrate the book world.

During these years, our family received an upright piano from someone as a gift. My father, who liked to go out and make music with two friends of his in the evenings, also acquired a large, heavy, and expensive tape recorder, a thing unknown to anyone else we knew. This was a family without a television set. Yet we had this tape recorder, a strong indicator of my father's values.

I pecked away at music on the piano, desperate to make music, and as unable to do it as I was unable to read.

On the tape recorder, I made "radio programs." I wrote them or recited the voices extemporaneously, I don't recall. I remember one long play I wrote involved the piano and my younger sister, who was persuaded by me to play a blind pianist who, gaining her sight, asks to be made blind again. The world was beautiful when she was blind, she said. And seeing the world had taken away the beauty. I think my parents were a good audience for this particular program. I wrote another about being abducted by aliens and taken into a strange spaceship and then escaping from it. There was a favorable response to this as well.

My father used the tape recorder sometimes to record radio programs, and one of these was the last act of the opera *Carmen,* being broadcast by the Metropolitan Opera in New York. We listened to this last act of *Carmen,* including Milton Cross' passionate reading of what was happening in the act, over and over again as I grew up.

My father listening to the opera on Saturday afternoons was a delightful part of our world. He would sit at a table in the back bedroom working on his wood carvings, and the sounds of the opera would fill the house. I loved the voice of Milton Cross, who always read a synopsis of the action before each act, with great and elegant expression. And I associate all of this with sheer happiness, with the breezes flowing through the open windows, even with the rain falling, with the windows filled with the green of the surrounding trees.

These were the ingredients of my education that had lasting effect.

Another notable aspect of my education was that I went all the way through the eighth grade being schooled only with girls. For two years I experienced a coeducational Catholic high school, and that was a different experience altogether, as I had become a teenager and become interested in "boys." After that I went to a Catholic girls' academy for a year, and then, after our family moved to Texas, I experienced a real true American public school. It was a fine, decent suburban school.

It's probably worth noting that I went on to an all-girls college, Texas Woman's University, and remained there for one school year, and one long summer, during which I took enormous course loads and worked full-time in the evenings to support myself. I was utterly desperate to get a college education, and after one year and two summer sessions, I had almost enough course credits to be a college junior.

It was on this college campus that my life became happy, really happy. We were treated as adults. The confusion and humiliation I associated with childhood came to an end.

I took to the freedom of college, and to navigating amid interesting classes and lecturers; and I responded strongly to complete lectures which enabled me to learn without the necessity of cumbersome and difficult books. The classes in sociology and in journalism and in music appreciation were particularly illuminating. The classes in English were discouraging. I made less-than-perfect grades because I wasn't considered an effective writer. And the atmosphere of the English classes was disciplinary and confining.

"We may assume," said the teacher, "that there are no Hemingways or Faulkners in this classroom. Therefore we expect you to write in decent sentences." I loathed the very idea of assuming mediocrity. I barely got by.

The one story I submitted to the college literary magazine was rejected. I was told it wasn't a story.

But these weren't defining experiences for me.

In the fifth grade, I'd written a novel which my schoolmates had read with great interest. And in the seventh grade, after seeing the film *King Solomon's Mines,* I wrote another novel in longhand which my classmates loved too. I wrote some short stories, and I attempted to write other grander longer works.

I was able to sink into my writing in a way that I could not do with books. I wrote fast, and my work had a penchant for character and action. What style it had I don't recall.

People were impressed with these compositions of mine, but there was no real place for this type of creative writing in my world. It was not something rewarded in the classroom. It happened on the margins, and the good responses to it were not something that involved the teachers. In fact, I sort of kept it secret from my teachers, and when I did attempt original writing, in response to an assignment, the results weren't so good.

All during these years, I struggled to do something significant, usually with music, or with reading. And I was not a success.

Not only had I pecked away at the piano, and struggled to learn some simple songs on my own, I'd also fallen in love with the violin. As a young teenager I wanted desperately to learn to play it, as there was no sound like it for me on earth. I'd heard Isaac Stern play the Beethoven Concerto for Violin and Orchestra at the Municipal Auditorium and this had been one of the transformative experiences of my life. I bought a violin at a pawnshop, with money given me by my father, and I struggled painfully hard to learn to play it. A kindly teacher at Loyola University even offered to give me lessons at no cost, but she was candid about my lack of ear and lack of general talent. She promised me that if I stuck with it, I could play well enough for the orchestra someday. But I wanted to be a virtuoso. And I found the discipline overall too difficult and finally gave it up.

Later on, I wrote novels about people who are shut out of life for various reasons. In fact, this became a great theme of my novels—how one suffers as an outcast, how one is shut out of various levels of meaning and, ultimately, out of human life itself.

I recall that I was shut out of the realm of music by my lack of talent, and I was shut out of book learning, and also, in a real way, I was not part of the world of the child.

I came out of my education with no sense at all of gender, and no liking whatsoever for being a child.

I can't say that Catholic education in all girls' schools made me a genderless person, because obviously thousands of girls went to Catholic schools and they didn't come out of the experience with no sense of gender. And many of them probably understood childhood and how to be children perfectly well enough.

But I emerged from these years with no clear sense of either one, and most likely because I did not get a sense of either one at home. If you are named Howard, if you grow up calling your parents by their first names, if you are raised to believe you can do just about anything you set your mind to, if you are never around "a superior gender" which takes precedence over you in anything, well perhaps you'll grow up having no sense of gender. But I would say that my lack of gender understanding transcends even these influences.

I had no sense then of being a feminine person, or indeed of being a masculine person. I did not identify with girls. I did not know boys.

And I felt extremely uncomfortable being called a child. I didn't fit as a child. I didn't "get" what childhood was. And I was a failure as a child. I knew I was. I made blunders with other children. I couldn't really speak their language. They knew something was "wrong" with me. They never trusted me and I didn't blame them. I didn't fit.

In retrospect, I feel the adults I knew did not give me a clear understanding of what a child was, and why anybody would want to be one.

I am not trying to be humorous.

As I look back on it, the state of childhood was regarded by adults of this time with suspicion, and there was a slight criminal taint to being a child. I resented this and refused to acknowledge it. I didn't agree that children had to be controlled, taught, restrained, disciplined, and above all made to do dull and boring things ad nauseam because this is what they deserved.

I didn't like other children, and I did not identify with them in any general war on adults.

I certainly didn't think I was guilty of any crime in being a child, or really that any other child was guilty of any crime, and I deeply detested the fact that we were treated as though we were guilty of weakness, sneakiness, poor ambition, general ignorance, and that we were being punished for this by the routines of our life, by the daylong prison of school, by the year-in and year-out confinement with some forty other persons, and by the intolerable burdens of written homework which was supposed to devour our free evening hours, and that this would go on until we grew up.

No disaster of my adult life ever equaled the misery and sometime hopelessness of childhood, as far as I'm concerned.

At no time did I feel as frustrated, as angry, as useless, as cut off from the real world as I did as a child. Huge blocks of my childhood were shameful wastes of time.

The slow deterioration of my mother led to the feeling of powerlessness. Indeed, around me I saw much deterioration. New Orleans was an inefficient, crumbling city in which garbage was piled in open heaps or cans on the curb every day. The French Quarter had a smell one caught two blocks away. Gutters were filled with litter. Great old houses were marked for demolition because it was believed they could not be maintained in the present era. Magnificent mansions here and there were replaced by hideous modern apartment build-ings. Along St. Charles Avenue, splendor and ruin coexisted on almost every block.

I wanted to escape this soft, endless drift towards ruin.

Because I unconsciously identified with adults, and pre-ferred to be with adults, I was mortified and insulted by them when they ignored me, patronized me, or degraded me, and I couldn't wait for this strange purgatorial state to come to a natural end. Let me repeat: my mother treated me as a person, not as a child. My father pretty much did the same thing. My sisters were interesting people to me, not children per se. But all this happened in the highly special world of our own household, with its disorder and its secrets, and its inevitable griefs.

I roamed around the city of New Orleans on foot or by bus and streetcar. And I did go all over the city, sometimes alone, and sometimes with a friend who liked to walk as much as I did. In fact, I walked all the time for the sheer joy of it, and riding the streetcar was dreamtime. In my wanderings, I became obsessed with architecture. I would stand for long moments contemplating some ruined house, dreaming of its restoration, dreaming of an adulthood in which I would live in some splendid building and restore it to grandeur, but how I didn't know.

The great things I remember from school were incidental. I loved the Girl Scout troop to which I belonged in fifth and sixth grades, and remember the ladies who formed it with great affection, and during our times at camp, I experimented with writing plays for the other girls and acting in these plays. I simply loved this; and I remember vaguely that we did plays at recess in school too. That was very simply great.

I also remember our seventh-grade teacher, Sister Francesca, reading a novel to us in the afternoons. It was called *Red Caps and Lilies,* and it was about young children during the French Revolution and their adventures as they roamed about Paris during those troublesome times. I don't remember a single thing from this novel, but I do remember the pleasure of listening to this story, and I remember, too, that other girls loved it, and that when Sister was reading this story to us just about everyone was happy. There was peace in the room.

I should add here that up until the age of fourteen I was a seriously religious child.

At twelve, I wanted to become a priest. When I was told that was impossible, I couldn't grasp why. I remember pestering a priest named Father Steffens about this, and that he tried to make swift work of the explanation by telling me that not only could I not be a priest, but there had actually been a time when theologians weren't sure women had souls.

I think he was being humorous when he said this, and in a way he was murmuring to himself about this more than he was talking to me. But there was some connection in his mind between this theological matter and my not being able to be a priest.

He was in many respects a patient and loving man, and he worked hard for our parish. I pestered him with my rampant enthusiasms. But I really didn't see why I couldn't be a priest. In fact, I was pretty certain that sooner or later I could become one. It was just a matter of patience, because at twelve, I didn't have enough power to swing it. But the time would come later on.

But I never forgot Father Steffens having said this, about theologians debating whether or not women had souls. I never forgot it yet it made no impression. I had no sense of being a young woman, or of being excluded from anything because of gender. The words seemed pointless and stupid and irrelevant. Yet I filed them away somewhere in my mind.

And I decided that I wanted to be a nun.

My plans did not work out, and with reason. I was no more suited to go into the convent than I was to go from prison to Solitary Confinement. The most important sort of nun was a contemplative nun, a nun who might become a great mystic, and I was not cut out for the cloistered life. I lost interest soon enough.

But I want to describe one important experience before I leave this aborted plan.

For one entire summer of my life, probably between the fifth and sixth grade, I worked every day from 5:30 in the morning to 6:00 p.m. in the evening at a home for elderly people run by the Little Sisters of the Poor. I happened into this experience because of my sister, Alice, who had been going there to work as well. To work in such a place was commendable Catholic volunteer behavior, and I took to this with great enthusiasm, and lived an extraordinary summer as the result of it.

The convent was on Prytania Street, and like many convents, it was made up of a central building, which included the chapel, and two great wings. It was three stories high. And it was red brick. The property included the entire city block. One wing housed the elderly women; the other housed the elderly men, and the convent proper where the nuns lived. All the rooms of the building were immense; the old people slept in huge dormitories. The hallways were extremely wide. Light flooded in from windows everywhere. Doorways had glass transoms. The old people roamed many large comfortable sitting rooms on the main floors. The place was orderly and clean.

Morning began with Mass at five-thirty in the chapel, and the chapel, like all the Catholic chapels I knew, was exquisitely beautiful, with the requisite carved pews, ornate altar, and opulent flowers on the linen-draped altar at all times.

The workday involved the care of the elderly at three meals which were served in the refectories on either side of the central building, the making of beds and dust mopping of the dormitories in which the old ladies lived, and some work in the infirmary where the bedridden were kept in long rooms, and some work in the laundry where I spent time with Sister Pauline, a Chilean nun, ironing clothes or working a mangler for the pressing of men's shirts and sheets.

Sister Ambrosine, an elderly French sister, managed the old ladies. At noon, a young sister, Sister Ignatius, came to help with the serving of the food.

This was a distinctly European place. And its architecture and atmosphere were apparently replicated not only all over America, but perhaps all over the world.

I loved working with all these sisters, but the most deliriously happy times were spent with Sister Pauline. She told me fabulous tales of growing up in Chile, and she also had a great love of the garden, and I went with her to cut marguerites, or white-petaled daisies, to put into vases for the many statues of the Virgin and the saints which were all over the convent.

These experiences in the garden were rapturous. It seemed there was a whole field there of white daisies through which we roamed. And beyond, the garden stretched the full length of the block, ending at the back walls. There was a long row of fig trees, a veritable orchard. Sister Pauline and I climbed up into these trees, and gathered figs for the old people. And it seemed we could move through these trees along these thick smooth branches, without ever climbing down to the ground.

In the infirmary, I wrote letters for the bedridden old people. I did many other chores. The nuns pretty much let me try anything that I wanted to try. What impressed me was the ease with which things could be accomplished or maintained in this environment. Caring for the old people was a noble and interesting task. And I loved old people.

I wanted to join the order. I begged my father to let me join. But he said no. He told me that he needed me at home and that I was trying to run away from being needed. And I knew that he was right. I sought a refuge in the coherent and intense life of this convent, in its great physical beauty, and in the gentle orderly ways of the nuns.

My father also told me that none of my talents would be of use to the Little Sisters of the Poor. It was not the order for me. In spite of my poor grades, it seemed I was perceived as having a great interest in music, books, and writing. And I think he was right that my temperament was not for the Little Sisters of the Poor. After all I was a person of rampant enthusiasms and dreams, of great frustration and longing, though how I was going to realize any dream was not clear.

My father told me another thing that summer. He said he was worried about me, that I was putting in a full day of work, and indeed a day of work that was as hard as his day. And I was not an adult, I was a child.

This was of course just what I loved about this summer. I was working, working with other adults, and in a realm of adults, where there were no children, and what I did had integrity. I was a part of a meaningful world.

When the summer came to an end, I went back to school, though I preserved my dream of being a nun someday in some order, and of being a saint, like the saints whose lives I read all the time.

Shortly after that, the home of the Little Sisters of the Poor on Prytania Street, this beautiful brick building with its gorgeous gardens, was torn down. It could not meet the fire codes of the period and it had to go. The old people were scattered to other homes, and I assume the nuns were too. And the building was soon obliterated and replaced by a modern building, as if the lovely coherent world there had never existed. It was a chilling loss.

I retain one key memory from that period. One evening I left the convent as usual and headed for the streetcar stop to take the car home. It was just one of many such evenings, with the sun still burning in the rapidly changing sky. On this particular evening as I walked up Prytania Street to Amelia Street, I caught sight of a huge tree, against the golden light, with its branches catching the breeze. The breeze took hold of the tree, limb by limb, and finally the entire tree, with its countless tiny curling leaves, was moving as if in a great dance.

I knew perfect joy then as I looked at that tree. I knew a joy that was beyond description. All was right with the world. The world made sense. God made us and God loved us; and I'd done a good day's work with the best people I knew and for the best reasons I knew; and here was this magnificent spectacle, this entrancing vision of this simple common tree caught in the simple common miracle of the evening breeze.

I was transported in that moment. No sorrow, no worry, no frustration, meant anything. It was a glorious moment, and I think of it all the time.

Move forward in time eighteen years. I'm a continent away from that spot and that moment; I'm an adult, an atheist. I live in Berkeley, California. I'm married, and I have a beautiful child. I am coming home one evening from the grocery store to our apartment.

And suddenly I look up and see another tree catch the breeze, just as that long-ago tree had done. This is an acacia tree of huge dark branches, and myriad leaves. And the sky is red with evening, and the light is going away. But the tree catches the wind and goes into this great transformative dance.

I stop and stare at this. I watch it. And I think of the long-ago tree in New Orleans outside the convent. And I feel the same sudden transporting joy. Life has meaning. Life has meaning just because this tree is so breathtakingly beautiful and because it can dance this way in the evening breeze. I am filled with happiness. I have no questions.

The next day in Berkeley, California, a man comes to the door and tells me that they are cutting down that acacia tree. I hear the buzz saws in the background. He is sorry, he says, but it is bringing down the telephone wires. There is nothing to be done. By the time I go out the tree is just about gone. All of it, all of that mighty tree, cut to pieces and gone.

Later that year my daughter is diagnosed with acute gran-ulocytic leukemia, and she begins to die.

One might ask, Was the moment of seeing that acacia tree a reminder? Was it perhaps a gentle whisper: Remember this: There are dark times coming. Remember this tree and its movements, its abandon, its surrender to the wind. Remember the tree you saw that evening when you were a child. *Remember the joy.*

5

WHAT DOES IT MEAN TO GROW UP CATHOLIC?

I entered school in 1947. I left Catholic high school in 1958.

Throughout these years I lived among other Catholics, in a large parish, and just about everyone I knew was Catholic, except for the teachers at the art museum in City Park. What they were I didn't know.

As I've mentioned, our parish had two immense and ornate churches, filled with emblems and tokens of our faith, and a small chapel in the Garden District, "for the rich people," to which we also went.

Our parish had a history. My father and mother had been born in it. Their parents had lived all their lives in it. And it encompassed a special geography of its own, being that it included the richest neighborhood in New Orleans, the Garden District, as well as the Irish Channel, which was the poorest white neighborhood of which I knew.

The world was not only solidly Catholic with people crowding the churches for morning Mass every day, it was high spirited, and had its vitally important seasonal events. In fact, the entire city of New Orleans was involved with these seasonal events, because Mardi Gras was a distinctive part of New Orleans and Mardi Gras was rooted in the church calendar, which was a calendar of seasons in church time and in real time.

I stress this because religion in this world included the world.

Mardi Gras was a celebration which lasted about two weeks, involving beautiful night parades along St. Charles Avenue, of papier-mâché floats crowded with rich members of the Mardi Gras clubs, which were called Krewes, and these people, all costumed and glittering, threw glass- or wooden-beaded necklaces to the thousands of us who packed the streets to watch the parade. The parades were lighted in those days by flambeaux, or torchlights fueled by oil or kerosene, and these flambeaux were carried by black men who frequently danced to the music of the high school bands that walked in the parade between the floats and kept up a spirited and sometimes frightening drum cadence as the parade moved along.

The end of the Mardi Gras season came with Mardi Gras Day itself, or Fat Tuesday, the day before Ash Wednesday, which was the beginning of Lent.

For the vast majority of the people I knew—in fact, for all

of them—Mardi Gras parades and celebrations and the convivial gathering on Fat Tuesday had nothing to do with debauchery or getting drunk. Families came to the parades; children dressed in costume on the big day itself. Our house, being on the parade route, was a family gathering place, and relatives came and went on various nights and on Mardi Gras Day.

My mother put out a big ham surrounded by crackers for the company on Mardi Gras Day. Vendors sold roasted peanuts in small brown bags, two for a nickel. Others sold cotton candy and trinkets which we couldn't afford.

Crowds began gathering every evening for the night parade, as soon as it got dark. The flicker of the flambeaux on the tree branches terrified me. The drums terrified me. Nevertheless the spectacle was seductive and dazzling, and ultimately great fun.

Mardi Gras was part of life as it was supposed to be lived—a deliberate making merry before the penitential season of Lent. Mardi Gras was firmly part of the Catholic world. Sometimes I fear people outside of New Orleans don't grasp this. And people outside of Catholicism don't grasp how most feast days and festal celebrations are part of our faith.

On Ash Wednesday we went to church to receive a thumbprint of ashes on our foreheads. This was the reminder of "Dust thou art, and to dust thou shalt return." Lent was forty days, and adults fasted in Lent. They ate only part of what they ordinarily ate, though I don't remember the actual rules. We children all gave up something for Lent.

The forty days of Lent equaled the forty days that Jesus had fasted in the desert, when He'd been tempted by Satan. Fasting, giving something up, doing penance, performing a prescribed penance, were part of the Catholic way to be good.

We were all keenly conscious of the progress of Lent towards Holy Week and the special celebrations involved.

The Stations of the Cross were said every Friday in Lent. Palm Sunday began Holy Week with joy as this was the day that Jesus entered the city of Jerusalem to delirious crowds of people who cried, "Hosanna, blessed is He who comes in the Name of the Lord." People carried palm branches when they did this, and they laid down their palm branches for the donkey carrying the Lord on the road.

Then came Spy Wednesday when Judas had gone off to betray Our Lord, and Holy Thursday on which the Lord's Supper occurred. On that day, as I recall, we received only Holy Communion, and there was no Mass. Legions of people trooped into church, went directly to kneel at the Communion rail, and received the Host.

On Good Friday, the day of Our Lord's death on the cross, there was no Mass either. One could go to the Stations of the Cross on that day, or go to longer more complex three-hour services during which all the lights were put out in the church at the moment that Our Lord actually expired. On Good Friday, people came to church all day long simply "to kiss the cross." Again the multitudes made their way to the Communion rail and knelt there, and the priest with the altar boy came along, the priest holding out a crucifix for each person to kiss. The altar boy or the priest wiped off the crucifix after each kiss.

It was our custom to visit nine churches on Good Friday and kiss the cross in each. One of the pure delights of living in New Orleans was that one could easily walk to nine Catholic churches. Indeed one had choices. I remember loving this devotion, in part because of the singular beauty of each church, and the special experience of entering and encountering a distinct sanctuary and a unique crucifix, and I also loved the fun of the walking on the way.

On Easter Sunday, we attended High Mass with magnificent choral music sung in Latin. The "Gloria" was definitely the most beautiful hymn. Even today at regular Sunday Mass, I love singing this hymn and will sing every verse of it, even if the cantor is only inviting us to sing the refrain. Of course today we are singing it in English, but let me give a taste of the Latin:

> *Gloria in excelsis Deo.*
> *Et in terra pax hominibus bonae voluntatis.*
> *Laudamus te.*
> *Benedicimus te.*
> *Adoramus te.*
> *Glorificamus te.*

This means "Glory be to God on high, and on earth peace to men of good will. We praise Thee; we bless Thee; we worship Thee; we glorify Thee."

In the Catholic Church of today, it goes like this:

Glory to God in the highest,
And peace to His people on earth.
Lord, God, heavenly King,
Almighty God and Father,
We worship You, we give You thanks,
We praise You for your glory.

It goes on and I could go on, but as I am talking now about New Orleans let me return to that theme.

Christmas in the time of my school days was even more sumptuous than Easter. In the early years, we didn't keep Advent, or the penitential four weeks before Christmas. So the Christmas Manger scene was erected quite early in each church, and it stood there resplendent for all to see for quite a number of days. I recall spectacular Manger scenes with very simply gorgeous life-size statues, and one particular statue of the Infant Jesus that couldn't help but fill me with happiness when I saw it. One can still buy a replica of this Baby Jesus today. He has dark wavy hair, quite a lot for a newborn, bright glistening eyes, and a lovely smile. His arms are extended and one of his knees is slightly raised. The baby looks absolutely overjoyed to be alive with us, to be one of us, to be a little person amongst human beings.

These Manger scenes were usually surrounded by Christmas greens and they smelled wonderful. They were usually built to one far side of the altar, but behind the Communion rail, so one could go up to the rail to kneel before them. And I suspect churches vied with one another for the most spectacular scene. There might be a structure to the stable or some other architectural feature. There were always statues of wooly haggard beast-laden shepherds and of the stalwart ox and the inevitable donkey who'd been there, and elegant statues of gowned angels with huge feathery white wings.

Mary knelt beside the Infant Jesus with her head bowed, almost always under a blue veil. Joseph, portrayed as an old man on account of tradition, knelt opposite, and sometimes he held his staff with one hand.

What I remember was the utter sweetness of the statues, the sublime scent of the greens, and other glittering decorative elements, all of this uplifting my spirits and filling me with a pure happiness that I associated with the entire season. The Manger scene remained up until January 6, which was the Feast of the Epiphany, or the day on which the Magi—the men from the East—came to visit the Divine Child. Then the exotic and detailed statues of these three wise men and sometimes statues of their beasts and their servants would be added to the tableaux. There was always at least one camel. And I think there was usually a little boy.

Of course we had Manger scenes in our individual classrooms at school, as well as Christmas trees, and we had Manger scenes in our homes under our living room Christmas trees as well. And the people of New Orleans constructed enormous and elaborate outdoor Manger scenes which drew crowds during the evenings by car and on foot.

As I recall there was a house on the corner of Washington and St. Charles that always erected a breathtaking Manger scene, and another house on Louisiana Avenue and St. Charles that erected a huge one as well. These were highly elaborate affairs, and it was fun to walk along the avenue in the evening and visit these particular Mangers as well as any others that people had erected to be seen.

One year one of our teachers created imaginative little Christmas worlds in the deep windowsills of our classroom. I remember that this sister laid down cotton for snow and put down little drugstore hand mirrors to make lakes in the snow. I suppose there were tiny little figures everywhere, rushing and skating, but I only remember that I loved these little universes and I thought this sister a wonderful person for having done this. Sisters were proprietary about their classrooms; each classroom had individual paintings and special touches, and sometimes even special collections of old books.

Even Christmas shopping was part of this festive and holy time of year. For me, it was a matter of roaming five-and-dime stores on Canal Street for the simple little presents I could afford. But I well remember the Christmas carols playing in every store I entered, and the gorgeous Christmas windows of the fine stores, Maison Blanche and D. H. Holmes. It seems to me in retrospect that the department stores and the dime stores did an excellent job of extending the "sacred space" of Christmas in those days. And I sometimes wonder whether for people of no religion, this might have been the only sacred space they knew. When people rail now against the "commercial nature of Christmas," I'm always conflicted and unable to respond. Because I think those who would banish commercialism from the holiday fail to understand how precious and comforting the shop displays and music can be.

I recall a saturation at Christmastime. It seemed the whole world was celebrating the birth of Christ. We were singing hymns in the classroom, and in church. We heard them everywhere we went. It was surely my favorite religious season. I remember sitting in the living room of our house, by myself, with only the lights of the Christmas tree for illumination, and looking lovingly at our tiny Manger scene with the devoted Virgin, the tiny Child, and St. Joseph at His side. We always went to Midnight Mass on Christmas, and Midnight Mass was unfailingly magnificent. True, I do remember the presents and caring much too much about them, but what I remember more than anything else was the immensity of the feast, and the awesome sense of meaning that permeated every aspect of it. Yes, we wanted gifts, but we wanted to give gifts as well. There was nothing like Christmas. Not even Mardi Gras exceeded Christmas in importance, and my child's mind sought some understanding of the mystery I was experiencing in the haunting Celtic carols we sang.

In my later years, bleak years, years without God, there were two films shown on television every Christmas which became of remarkable importance to me. One was *It's a Wonderful Life* with Jimmy Stewart and Donna Reed; and the other was *Scrooge*, Dickens' *Christmas Carol*, starring Alastair Sim. Year after year I waited anxiously for these films, and sometimes they were the only Christmas films offered on national television, and I cannot help but wonder how important they must have been to people everywhere who were trying to regain that deep mystery of Christmas, in a world that no longer perhaps believed in it, or was determined to blot it out. Both films are as popular as ever today. *It's a Wonderful Life* seems to be about American ambivalence to Christmas, and the desperate need to reaffirm the values of the season, no matter how bleak and impoverished the holiday season has become. As for Scrooge, he is Dickens' great and masterly judgment on the miser and swindler in each of us. In our house, when we gather for Christmas, we still watch both these films. It is a judgment on us as a nation that we seem unable to produce more films of this caliber and meaning, especially given the dazzling new cinematic resources at our command. Some years, Christmas simply doesn't happen on American television. And it doesn't happen in the movies either. This is a source of anxiety and disappointment to me. I fear our loss of sacred space and time. I dream of making beautiful and profound and magnificent Christmas films.

Back to childhood: as I grew older, somebody or some group of people in the church decided that we should observe the Advent season, and so the cribs could not be placed in the churches until Christmas Eve. Because in America "nothing is more over than Christmas," this meant that the cribs didn't command anybody's attention for very long. The radiant Christ Child came and went in a matter of a few days. This was a terrible loss. However, the celebration of Advent was an interesting idea in itself, involving an Advent wreath with four candles for the Sundays of Advent. But I mourned the days when the Manger scenes went up early and the sheer joy of the Christmas season went on for a long, long time.

After January 6, children in the Irish Channel and possibly in other neighborhoods too gave King cake parties. A cake was baked with a tiny statue of a king in it; the person at the party who got the piece of cake with the king in it had to give the next party. I associated this entirely with the Feast of Epiphany, but as Christmas season ran into Mardi Gras season, somehow the King cake parties became intimately associated with Mardi Gras, and King cakes are now sold all over New Orleans, and sent all over the world from New Orleans, at Mardi Gras time.

King cakes are huge oval cakes laid out on stiff cardboard, and covered with sticky brightly colored icing. There is nothing so sweet and sticky as a King cake. The cakes have tiny babies hidden in them now, not kings.

The other festival that was almost equal to Christmas in its splendor was the festival of the Virgin Mary in the month of May. Each parish in New Orleans and each school managed its tribute to the Virgin Mary in its own way.

In our parish, the procession and the May Crowning came at the end of the month. On the evening of the May Crowning all the schoolchildren assembled to walk in ranks through the streets of the parish, along with thousands of parishioners. If you were a little girl, you wore your old white Communion dress for at least three years. Girls who'd made their Confirmation wore their white Confirmation dresses each year for as long as they could. The members of various organizations carried statues in the procession. When I was in high school, the Legion of Mary carried the statue of Our Lady of Fatima in the procession, and my sister, who was a member, walked along beside the bier saying her rosary with the other high school girls.

The scent of flowers was everywhere during these processions.

I can't imagine how long this procession was, and I don't remember any set route. But it took us all through the packed streets of the Irish Channel, and I remember one year noticing that house after house had its own glorious shrine to the Virgin in a front window or on a front porch. People came down in the dusk to say their rosaries with us as we passed. I'm sure we sang hymns too. But I don't recall singing hymns until we all returned to the enormous school yard for the crowning of the Virgin there.

This was done with a life-size statue; and I can recall standing with thousands of people in the yard, amid so many white lilies that the air was drenched with their perfume. There seemed to be banks and banks of lilies before the Virgin.

The priest would speak a sermon, sometimes a long one, and then the May Court of several teenage girls in lovely evening gowns would prepare for the crowning itself. One girl was always chosen to put the crown onto the Virgin's head. Two traditional hymns were always sung. One was tender and almost sad:

On this day, O beautiful Mother,
On this day we give thee our love.
Near thee, Madonna, fondly we hover,
Trusting thy gentle care to prove.

The second hymn, we sang with considerably more spirit, and it was during this hymn that Our Lady was in fact crowned with a crown of woven flowers.

Bring flowers of the rarest
Bring flowers of the fairest
From garden and woodland and hillside and dale,
Our full hearts are swelling,
Our glad voices telling
The praise of the loveliest rose of the dale!
REFRAIN:
O Mary we crown thee with blossoms today!
Queen of the Angels, Queen of the May.
O Mary we crown thee with blossoms today,
Queen of the Angels and Queen of the May.

When I went to Holy Name of Jesus School uptown, we had a May Crowning every school day in the basement, right after the noon recess. Each grade had its turn to crown the Blessed Mother, with the same traditional hymns and certain prayers that were always said.

Much later, during my first year of college, and my first year as an atheist, I missed the May Crowning so much that one evening I bought a huge bouquet of flowers and I went out alone on a grassy slope beside the dormitory and sang these hymns to the Virgin, and, lying on the grass, amongst the flowers, I cried and cried.

In the month of July, our parish had what it called the Bazaar. This lasted for several nights in the school yard, and there were many booths set up with games of chance. One put one's money on a number on the long counter of the booth, and then the wheel was spun. I was considered lucky and won chocolate cakes for a nickel more than once. An automobile was raffled off, and for days beforehand we sold raffle tickets to raise money for the school. There was a bar at the Bazaar where men sat drinking beer and talking, and it was great fun to go. There must have been more things to do. I don't remember them. I remember the strings of lights over the school yard, the brightness, the sense of festivity, and also the sense that I didn't really know many people in my parish—as I came from St. Charles and Philip, a world away—but that the people knew each other.

When I'd gone to birthday parties in the Irish Channel, I'd received the same impression. I really didn't know these people, but they all knew each other. They were part of something. I wasn't part of it. And I think this was a fairly accurate appraisal.

My parents were what I would call First Generation Intellectuals. They loved literature and classical music. They wanted to some extent to separate themselves from the "old neighborhood" of the Irish Channel, and they did. They spoke proper English, and had great dreams for their children. And we were set apart due to the way that we spoke—with no discernible neighborhood accent—and by our constant exposure to opera and classical music, and to books and to art.

We didn't feel at home with children who made fun of us and called us "brains," as in "You're a brain!"

But my intent here is to discuss the great religious world in which I was brought up. And that did not necessarily involve my particular psychological trials.

We all felt very much a part of the Catholic Church, a part of our parish churches, and part of the church throughout the world. We knew that New Orleans was a distinctly Catholic city. And the name of our archbishop of the time was mentioned as frequently as the name of the mayor.

We saw our archbishop at Confirmation when he sealed each individual child's forehead with holy oil.

But we heard about him all the time.

Now and then he would tell us that it was a mortal sin to go to see a particular film. I recall this happening with the film *Baby Doll.*

This was not particularly upsetting because in general we followed the advice of the Legion of Decency on all films and there were always films being condemned.

We knew the Legion of Decency was national. It was our guide as to what was appropriate and what was not. We went through life ignoring such films as *Salome: The Dance of the Seven Veils* starring Rita Hayworth or *And God Created Woman* with Brigitte Bardot. But there were many interesting films that we could see.

Our entire school went to see Cecil B. DeMille's *The Ten Commandments* and this was a marvelous experience for us all. I went back to see the film on my own. The sheer energy and faith of the film were overwhelming and uplifting. I've seen the film countless times since, including recently, and I am still in awe of what it accomplished for a mass audience. There is no one in the world of 2008 making films like Cecil B. DeMille.

If I could be something other than what I am today, I would like to be a movie producer, like Cecil B. DeMille, making religious films. I would love to have a studio which did nothing but make giant religious spectacles with the finest actors, directors, and cinematographers available. I would love to remake *Quo Vadis,* and *The Robe,* and maybe even *Ben-Hur.* I would love to bring a whole new generation of biblical epics to the screen. I dream of this. I dream of somebody doing it! After all, it doesn't really have to be me.

On another occasion, the whole school went to the theater to see a foreign film about Our Lady of Fatima, and her appearances to three Portuguese children. We were deeply and suitably impressed. It seems we all went to see a film called *Sally and Saint Anne* with Ann Blyth, but my memory of that is less clear.

Film was part of my family life. And film was, in the main, wholesome and agreeable, and enjoyed by just about everybody.

I remember seeing *On the Waterfront* with my father, and noting that the film interested him very much. There was a priest in the film played by Karl Malden, who actually punches a guy, and then drinks a beer. This priest also smoked cigarettes. He was a virile, regular guy type of priest—that was the whole point of the cigarettes and the beer—and a hero on the side of the workingmen in the film who were struggling against the corrupt bosses of the union.

This priest was true to the priests that we knew in real life. They didn't punch people in the nose or drink beer, but they were big beefy workingmen and they worked hard day in and day out with the people of the parish, as I've mentioned above.

In the Redemptorist Rectory, where they lived, no layperson could go beyond the private doors. The rectory contained the office behind a barred window where one could go to get a copy of a baptismal certificate or ask to see a particular priest. I don't recall ever going into the rectory for anything without seeing priests in the conference rooms on both sides of the little hallway, talking to adults. I had a sense of priests working with couples young and old on family matters, and there were always men around the rectory or the church as well as women. In fact, there might have been more men than women.

Every year our church celebrated a special novena to a particular Redemptorist saint. This was St. Gerard Majella, who had been a Redemptorist in life. There were statues of him in our churches, and there were boys all over the parish named after him, and perhaps there were girls named Geraldine.

The novena ran nine nights (as a string of nine services or observances is what defines a formal novena), and the church on those nights was packed with men and women, with people standing outside on the steps and in the street.

We sang a passionate hymn to St. Gerard that ran something like:

> *O sainted Gerard, e'er protect us*
> *While through this vale of tears we roam.*
> *In doubts and trials e'er direct us,*
> *And lead us to our heavenly home.*

All of the hymns I've described were songs to us as children that we sang when walking in the evening, or riding in the car. We sang hymns like "O Lord, I Am Not Worthy" right after singing "I've Been Working on the Railroad" or "My Darling Clementine."

Up in the austere but magnificent church of the Holy Name of Jesus we sang a hymn that fitted the grandeur:

> *Holy God, we praise Thy name,*
> *Lord of all, we bow before Thee!*
> *All on earth Thy rule acclaim,*
> *All in heav'n above adore Thee;*
> *Infinite Thy vast domain,*
> *Everlasting is Thy reign.*
> *Infinite Thy vast domain,*
> *Everlasting is Thy reign.*

That too was a family favorite.

As I grew up in this world, I felt completely safe and secure in my Catholic identity, and I never sensed any conflict between my world as a Catholic and the world around me. I've learned since that this was a strong period for Catholics in America, when parish life all over the nation was vigorous, and when convents and monasteries were full. Lots of men were still entering the seminaries to become priests. And girls wanted to become nuns.

This was a time when the Catholic Church was deeply respected in America. It was a cultural force. Priests all over America were associated with social justice, with the workingman and his rights. Our influence in Hollywood with the Legion of Decency was respected influence. And the name of Bishop Fulton J. Sheen was a household word.

We'd grown up listening to Monsignor Sheen on the radio. And after that, he became a television star.

I had no way of knowing that this was a world that would soon change dramatically and entirely for a variety of complex reasons.

It fell apart for me before any great change happened in it—simply because I was growing up; I was becoming extremely curious and conflicted about sex; and I was also becoming curious about "the modern world." I was making interesting friends; I had heard talk of the Beat Generation. In a friend's house I'd found an informative stack of *Time* magazines. This provided a treasure trove of information about life outside New Orleans. But the Beats, in particular, were my focus. I had no conception that anyone might think these bohemians of New York and San Francisco were immoral. They were artists; they wrote poetry. For me, they held spiritual values. They did great things.

In the summer after my freshman year of high school, my

mother finally died of the drink. Even now I remember the day with a palpable sense of horror. Her final drinking spell had been, perhaps, the longest ever, and when my younger sister came down with appendicitis, my father felt that we were needed at the hospital, and that my mother couldn't be left at home alone. My mother had sometimes fallen when she was drunk; and more than once she had dropped a cigarette and set a mattress on fire. My father called her closest cousins to come get her, and take care of her; and the last time I saw my mother, she was being led down the garden path to the gate, begging my father not to do this, not to give her over to this cousin; she didn't want her cousins to see her as she was.

Within a matter of hours the call came: she wasn't moving or speaking. The priest came rushing up our back steps, in his black cassock, beads rattling, and I had to head him off and send him to the car that was ready to take him to the cousin's house uptown. My mother was dead before he got there. Nevertheless he anointed her, gave her the Last Sacraments, as we called them, and assured everyone that no one knows precisely when the soul leaves the body. Perhaps she had been reached by the Saving Grace in time.

When the word reached me, I went to church. I remember going to the shrine of Our Mother of Perpetual Help and trying to talk to her. But I was numb. I was unable to form coherent words. I was relieved that my mother's long struggle was over. I was relieved that our long struggle was over. I was elated and yet speechless with a kind of terror. I knew that our lives would not be the same.

The ghastly moment at the funeral came when they closed the coffin. I began to cry uncontrollably. And I still remember standing over her grave in St. Joseph's Cemetery, surrounded by mourners, and thinking that all the world was gray, and that the daily light I'd once taken for granted would never return.

Two years later, in 1957, my family moved from New Orleans, and we might as well have been entering America for the first time when we arrived in Dallas, Texas.

My father's new wife was a Baptist who struggled to be Catholic for my father's sake, even though to marry her—a divorced woman—he had made a tragic break with his own church.

My faith was unchanged. Even a year in an extremely old-fashioned boarding school had not really tested it. And it proved as strong in a makeshift cafeteria church in Richardson, Texas, as it had been all along.

After all, the Catholic Church was supposed to be the same everywhere, and always and for everyone. And it seemed to me that it was. Even in a suburban school cafeteria, the Mass was in Latin, and at the moment of the Consecration, Christ was beneath our roof, and the sermons were very much the same. We had to remain the same.

I didn't know then that the Catholics of the early twentieth century were decidedly and deliberately and consciously anti-modern, that they had been told to be against the modern world by the pope.

I knew nothing of recent church history at all. As I mentioned earlier, I had a better sense of what the Middle Ages had been like, and what the great heresies of the early centuries might have been, than of any recent developments in the Catholic Church.

For all I knew there were no recent developments in the Catholic Church. That was certainly the illusion we were supposed to believe and support. The Catholic Church survived all attacks and all crises, all persecutions and all assaults. The Protestant Reformation had not stopped it. Nothing ever would or could stop the church.

As Monsignor Fulton J. Sheen said in one of his Sunday evening broadcasts, "The church is a rock pitched into space."

My entire universe was steeped in styles of church art that were rococo, baroque, and Romantic, and these styles seemed to flow from the Greek classical styles I so much admired. This included not only the statues and pictures in church, but the poetry we read and the prayers we recited with their elegant use of "thee" and "thou."

There was a great continuity to our beliefs, to our life, our life within our Catholic city of New Orleans—and our life beyond it—a continuity to our art, our poetry, and our liturgy and our devotions and our prayers. It was a universe, this world in which I grew up Catholic. And the experiences of art and literature and music that penetrated it were interwoven with its values. It was a realm unto itself.

Pope Pius XII was the head of the Roman Catholic Church. And Pope Pius XII, as far as I knew, had been pope all my life.

There was criticism in our realm of the world beyond, but

this seemed logical and inevitable. The priests railed against divorce and remarriage from the pulpit. They declared in so many terms that we would "not come down off the cross" on this issue no matter what other religions did.

We also prayed for the death of Stalin. We prayed, I think, for an end to Soviet Communism and Soviet Russia which constituted a threat to the whole world.

In New Orleans, there had been criticism of television when it was first invented, dire warnings of how it would ruin the imagination of children who watched it, or how soap commercial jingles would replace revered family songs.

Our family held out against television for years. In our chaotic old house, furnished haphazardly with old bits and pieces of furniture, a materialistic and profane thing like television was regarded with deep suspicion.

Finally someone gave us a television, a monstrous table model of a wooden box with a tiny six-inch screen. At last we discovered what the rest of the world already took for granted. What a revelation it was to see Liberace, after hearing about him at school for years, and to find out who Sid Caesar really was.

We sat on straight-back chairs in the dining room to watch television. Old foreign films came on at night, passable English fare, it seemed. And my father watched the boxing matches, and I enjoyed watching them with him. All my life I've been a boxing fan.

My mother who had patiently endured all the clamor against television for many years pronounced it as the most wonderful entertainment one could bring into one's home. But we all knew our mother loved film, and sometimes it was said that up until she married, she'd seen every film ever made.

Television certainly didn't change our values.

Frequently in my house, people were denounced as "rank materialists" and there was ongoing discussion about the real dangers of Communism and how Communism might and could take over the United States. Families who limited the number of their children were spoken of as ruining America. Conformity was ruining America. But Communism was the greatest of all threats.

Senator Joe McCarthy was a hero to Catholics I knew. The only magazine ever delivered to our house was the *American Legion* magazine.

But I didn't care much about any of this. I didn't read the papers, any more than I read anything else. I knew nothing at all about recent history, and I had no interest in politics whatsoever. I moved in and out of enchanting periods of history in my passions and hobbies. I dreamed of being a bohemian; I dreamed of traveling to all the countries of the world.

Television certainly didn't make a mindless slave of me.

Even the new suburbs of Dallas, Texas, where I found myself for the last year of high school, did not make me a conformist, though it was rather dazzling to be in the America I had glimpsed on TV.

I headed towards college, filled with a sense of personal power. I could become a great writer. And we had a multitude of great Catholic writers. Their books had been all over our house as I grew up.

Yet within a short time, it was the modern world—wanting to know the great incidents and heroes and heroines of the world—more than sexuality—that eventually caused me to leave the church.

6

As I have mentioned, I came out of childhood with no sense of being a particular gender, and no sense of being handicapped by being a woman because I didn't believe I was a woman or a man.

Let me say briefly, because it's too painful to relate in any detail, that I learned all about gender in adolescence, even as I moved against gender distinctions and refused to accept gender limitations.

Plunged into a coeducational high school at fourteen, I soon caught on that there were tremendous liabilities to being a girl. There was no such thing as gender equality. No one had yet spoken the word "feminism," and my view of life soon involved negotiating my way through a minefield in which "good girls" could be destroyed. A raft of activities could result in one losing one's reputation, and at the very worst, one could get pregnant, have to give up the baby for adoption, or one's entire life might be destroyed.

In this rigid Catholic world, "going steady" with one boyfriend was a mortal sin. It was a case of deliberately putting oneself into the occasion of sin, and that was sin. My mind revolted against this, but I couldn't come up with satisfactory or enduring principles. Any kissing was a mortal sin. One might play something of a game with a boy involving only venial sin, but this was dangerous, as well as being socially necessary if one was to have any boyfriend at all. Rock-and-roll music took this little world by storm, and it was tolerated at our Catholic school dances, but much frowned upon by the priests and the nuns. Elvis Presley was regarded with rank suspicion, and it did seem finally that to be a successful American teenager, one had to walk a moral tightrope, with Hellfire beneath it, and no net.

I didn't like all this. I didn't like being a teenager any more than I liked being a child. I deeply resented that "a girl" could get a bad reputation because of the way she dressed. I thought this was inane and unjust. Just about all the rules that pertained to gender struck confusion in me, and none really converted me to any view that penalized a woman at the expense of a man in a pure moral sense. In sum, the society seemed confused. I didn't become confused.

The teenage state was, if anything, less desirable than that of a child. There was an even greater criminal taint attached to it apparently in the eyes of adults. And it seemed to me that most of what I heard about "youth" from adults was entirely negative, and to a large extent unconvincing and hypocritical.

I was told repeatedly, for example, that "youth was wasted on the young," but I retained the obdurate conclusion that my youth was not wasted on me at all, but was wasted on older people around me. I still believe this.

I passed through these adolescent years, with considerable misery, and with some happy experiences, but the lessons— that girls were responsible for keeping boys in line sexually, that good girls never gave in until the marriage night, that brides, pure as lilies, ought to want husbands who had acquired a little experience, that housework was noble and important, that marriage was to be desired over the single state, that one should have as many children as God chose to send to one—these lessons made little or no lasting impression on me. I remained a person in rebellion, and continued to gravitate to subjects beyond my immediate milieu.

I needn't linger on the blunders or trials of this period, except to say that religion became mixed up with it.

I think I lost my intimate conversation with God during this period. I think I stopped talking to Him and looking to Him to help me—long before I lost my faith.

It became almost impossibly difficult to disentangle the moral teachings of my church from all the "teachings" of the blue-collar class in which I was brought up as to what a "good girl" represented. I spent far too much mental energy trying to distinguish class values from core Catholic values, class traditions from genuine Christian truths. And I didn't achieve any success.

But never in my mind did God Himself become connected with gender, or the gender morass in which I found myself.

Never was I convinced that Jesus Christ, Our Lord, wanted me to be a certain kind of good blue-collar-class girl. My deepest convictions transcended gender. The God in whom I believed transcended gender. Reason and conscience and heart told me these things. Yes, God was He, but He was infinitely bigger than a man. God belonged to the wild and rambunctious female saints as surely as He belonged to the male saints. God's Blessed Mother was more important perhaps than any other person after God. And she was a woman, and a uniquely powerful woman. Not only was she uniquely powerful, she was uncompromised. In sum, power and blamelessness coexisted in her. God was immediate and absolute. Mass and Holy Communion were for everyone, old and young.

Yet life as an American teenager was penitential and excruciating. This was another half existence, rather like that of childhood. I wanted full existence. I dreamed of marrying young so as to be an adult; I dreamed of having a child young so as to be an adult. I dreamed of any sort of escape from the control of the adults around me who seemed to have contempt for all of us young people a priori, as if we were an offense to them for having been born.

I was just too confused, however, to make much of the whole struggle.

By my senior year in high school, I had a full-time job that kept me working school nights till 10:00 p.m., and all day on weekends, including Sunday. This made me happy. It seemed to have some value. I don't recall how I passed my classes. I think it was the same old formula: listen, seek to follow the spoken words, and write well on the exams. There certainly wasn't much time to read.

By the time I entered Texas Woman's University, I had earned and banked money for the entire first year's room and board and fees. I welcomed the genderless world of TWU, not because I knew it was genderless but because it was a serious place.

I wanted a meaningful and significant life.

I was already deeply in love with a high school boy named Stan Rice, but as he had his senior year to complete in Richardson, Texas, and did not seem to be in love with me, I was on my own. It's worth noting that my militant Catholicism had discouraged him. I couldn't engage in kissing and hugging because it was a mortal sin. I had committed a mortal sin in kissing and hugging him quite a lot, but I think the grief and the sense of catastrophe on my part, my misery over all of it, understandably put him off.

Of course the atmosphere of the university attracted me mightily. Over the years, I've found it impossible to explain to people who never went to college that college is too different from high school for the two to be compared.

In college, one is an adult, expected to select one's classes, and get to them, at various times, and in different buildings, on one's own. Different university departments immediately bring one into contact with scores of new people.

The prison of high school is indeed blasted to pieces, and one wanders in a "brave new world."

Perhaps it's worth noting in passing that an aunt who visited before I went to college strongly advised me to major in something much more realistic than journalism. She suggested secondary education so that I might be a teacher, as the idea of working for a newspaper and being a reporter or a writer was far-fetched. She made quite a case for normality, averring that highly intelligent people weren't happy. Her thinking was not unlike that of nuns who had urged me to be good in all subjects, rather than to try to excel in any one subject. I simply didn't agree with these people. And college was the place where I left all such thinking behind.

More than thirty years later, this aunt came to a jam-packed book-signing party for me in Kentucky, with an armload of my published novels for me to sign. I didn't remind her of that old conversation, in which she had so strenuously urged me to curb my ambition. But I think of it every time I see her. My life went a different way.

Let me return to the year 1959.

I landed at a secular campus in a Protestant part of the country, and among my many classmates and teachers there were no Catholics, and I soon found myself confronted with barriers to understanding the modern world that I felt I had to overcome.

The Index of Forbidden Books loomed over my head. More insidious than the Index itself, which contained many venerable classics, including all the works of Dumas except for *The Count of Monte Cristo,* was the concept of the "general index" which governed any book which was likely to lead a Catholic into the occasion of sin. In other words, you didn't have to find Albert Camus on a written index to know that you couldn't read Albert Camus. All you had to know was that he was an atheist and an existentialist. That made his work forbidden under pain of mortal sin.

In the world I'd left behind there had been much talk of the dangers of secular colleges. One teaching sister had told us in class that it was better for a Catholic not to go to college at all than to go to a non-Catholic college. My father had dismissed that notion out of hand.

So had I.

I needed a college education. My father and mother had not had college educations. I needed to work to become somebody. And there were no Catholic universities that I could conceivably afford.

There was also much talk in my late childhood of people "reading themselves out of the church." If you asked too much, read too much, questioned too much, you would wind up outside the church and it would be your own damned fault. I took that to heart, as I took everything I'd been taught as a Catholic. But I was hungry for knowledge, hungry for information, hungry for facts.

As I roamed in the library and the bookstore at Texas Woman's University in Denton, Texas, I began to lose heart.

Sexually, I was in an agony of strong desire and impossible curiosity. It was a mortal sin to have solitary sex; to kiss; to do anything basically except to have conjugal relations in marriage which were entirely open to procreation. So this was an undercurrent of constant pressure and pain.

But the question of the modern world became bigger and bigger to me with every passing day. The old world of New

Orleans was gone beyond reprieve, along with all its protective accoutrements, and I was no longer interested in it.

I wanted to read all the books I saw in Voertman's Bookstore, near the campus. I gazed at big thick trade paperbacks, with rich interesting covers, and names on them like Kierkegaard and Heidegger, Jean-Paul Sartre, Albert Camus, Immanuel Kant, and Aldous Huxley, and I wanted to know what was in those books. I wanted to read Nabokov's *Lolita,* even if it was a scandal. I wanted to see tantalizing and condemned foreign films.

My education, which had left off to some extent with my mother's death, resumed in earnest in college classrooms, as ideas poured forth from my professors on various topics ranging from sociological studies of American class structure to the preeminence of the style of the great writer Ernest Hemingway, who in our Catholic schools had been completely dismissed and ignored.

I was around students who knew much more of contemporary literature than I did, and who discussed subjects I'd never thought to discuss. They were hungry for learning, and there was no barrier to their learning. And they were good and wholesome people.

My faith began to crack apart.

All around me I saw not only interesting people, but essentially good people, people with ethics, direction, goals, values—and these people weren't Catholic. They negotiated their moral decisions with considerable thought but without the guidance, it seemed, of any established church. I liked them. I was learning from them, learning from fellow classmates as well as teachers, something which had not happened to me earlier in the purgatory of childhood where it seemed other children were monsters with precious little to teach.

Most of my new friends took sexual experiment rather casually. All girls were cautious in these times; pregnancy was the ever-present threat. Contraceptives could only be got from doctors and by married people. There was no birth control pill. Young women did not slip into affairs easily, but their reasons for this were practical, and they were as intimate as they felt it was safe to be, and they weren't tormented by notions of sin. They knew a great deal more than me about sexuality, and their attitudes seemed wholesome and natural. My ignorance of sexuality, in fact, became something of a running joke.

But the lust for the modern world was infinitely greater in me, I think, than the desire for sex. I ceased to believe that the Catholic Church was "the One True Church established by Christ to give grace." Those are the words of the *Baltimore Catechism,* and we were too far from the world of the *Baltimore Catechism* and things were working entirely too well.

I couldn't understand why so much vital information was beyond my Catholic reach.

I had at the time a spiritual director, a Paulist priest, at the church in Denton, Texas, and this man was fairly young, quite intelligent, and generous in trying to help me through what had become a nexus of utter pain.

We had many conversations on various matters, probably more about my sexual desires just to kiss and embrace a young man than anything else. But we also talked about my doubts. And doubts were beginning to tear me apart.

I remember at one point, a decisive point, the priest suddenly realized what he had not realized earlier: that I had grown up going to daily Mass and Communion, and had gone to Catholic schools almost all my life. He'd assumed apparently that I did not have that kind of old-fashioned upbringing. When it came clear to him that, indeed, I had come from that milieu, he said rather dramatically, "Oh well, if you were brought up like that, Anne, you'll never be happy outside the Catholic Church. You'll find nothing but misery outside the Catholic Church. For a Catholic like you, there is no life outside the Catholic Church."

He meant well when he said this. He was speaking, I think, from his experience with people. The year was probably 1960. I was eighteen going on nineteen, and, well, it was understandable what he said.

But when he said it, something in me revolted. I didn't argue with him.

But I was no longer a Catholic when I left the room.

Those few remarks had pushed me right over the edge.

It wasn't his fault.

But he had hit on something which I couldn't abide—the idea that my upbringing condemned me to be a Catholic forever, no matter what my heart and conscience told me was true.

My heart and my conscience were telling me to leave the church, to explore. My heart and my conscience wanted information. My heart and my conscience were in love with the wide world. Whether there was true knowledge out there, beyond the pale, I wanted to discover. I hungered for experience, for risk. And I also believed mightily in the life of the mind, and the life of the artist, though what kind of artist I might be, I didn't know.

The church had become for me anti-art and anti-mind. No longer was there a blending of the aesthetic and the religious as there had been throughout my childhood.

Desperately I sought to escape the sense of sin that seemed to dominate every choice facing me. I lost faith in Hellfire. Or to put it differently, faith in Hellfire simply did not hold me firmly, as faith in God had once done. I left the church.

I stopped going. I stopped being a Catholic. I stopped arguing with people about being Catholic. I stopped getting upset if they made fun of my church or the pope. I simply quit.

I quit for thirty-eight years.

The real tragedy however was that I quit believing in God. I think about this a great deal. People ask me why this happened; sometimes they indicate that my loss of faith must have been precipitated by some emotional or social event.

There was no emotional or social event. This was a catastrophe of the mind and heart.

I could not separate my personal relationship with God, and with Jesus Christ, from my relationship with the church. As I mentioned, I'd stopped really talking to God a long time ago. I hadn't felt entitled to talk to Him in a long while. I'd felt far too demoralized to talk to Him. I just wasn't the Catholic girl who had a right to talk to Him. I harbored too many profane ambitions. And now faith in Him was giving

way. I think I had to stop believing in God in order to quit
His church, and the pressure to quit became intolerable.

Whatever the case, I left it all.

I think I can safely say I never put my dilemma before
God. I never knelt down before Him and said, "Please help
me with this." I failed to perceive Him as a source of creative
solutions to one's personal problems. I failed to see Him as
a Person of Infinite Compassion. My religious mind was
an authoritarian mind, and once I found myself at odds
with God, I couldn't speak to Him. I couldn't question Him.
Instead I made decisions about Him. And they amounted to
rejection of His existence, and a determination to face the
world with a new courage which seemed right.

The church, with all its rules about sex, the modern world,
and books and matters of dogma, had become absolute proof
to me that God didn't exist. The idea of God belonged to the
utter falsity of Catholicism. If an edifice like that was a pack
of lies—and it had to be a lie that one could burn in Hell for
all eternity for masturbating or kissing a boy, or reading a
novel by Alexandre Dumas, or an essay by Sartre—then there
was no God.

There just couldn't be a God. A God would never have
made a church so unnatural and so narrow, and so seemingly
fragile—vulnerable to information, that is—as the Catholic
Church. People who believed in God believed in churches,
and churches told you lies. Not only did they tell you lies,
they made you tell lies. They taught you how to tell those
lies when you were a little child.

I had grown up telling lies for the Catholic Church. Let

me give one example. If those outside the church criticized the Inquisition and its torture of heretics or Jews, we had a standard Catholic answer, and it was this: The Inquisition was only going along with the times. Indeed the Inquisition never really executed anyone. It was the secular state that did the executing.

That, I think, is a first-rate Catholic lie.

But Catholics of my time were taught quite a number, and their goal was always the same—to gloss over the failings or corruption of the church and bring the subject of the discussion back to the church's perfection.

As I lost my faith in God and in this church, these many lies seemed proof to me that I was moving away from falsehood and into truth.

Also I'd come to realize what most Christians realize sooner or later—that millions were born and grew up and died without ever knowing anything of Christianity, and that seemed to prove that Christianity was only one man-made sect making grandiose claims that could not be true.

In my heart of hearts, I believed this finally: there was no God.

The cure for the agony of my religious upbringing was to face this fact, I felt, and to journey on bravely in spite of it, and to learn what was good and interesting and challenging from the teachers of the modern world who had long ago rejected God, out of necessity, yet never ceased to care bravely about the fate of human beings. And this caring was key. The secular humanists I knew did care. They were conscientious people.

In sum, outside the Catholic Church, one did not find a sinkhole of depravity. Quite to the contrary, one found articulate people who made complex and refined distinctions about how to be a good human being.

After a few months of dismal grieving for my faith, I began to feel a new relaxation, and a new passion for life. But I felt a certain bitter darkness too. The world without God was a world in which anything might happen, and there would never be justice for the millions who died at the hands of tyrants, or the poor who suffered in the neglected parts of the world. The world without God was the world of the Cold War in which "the bomb" might drop at any minute—and civilization might be annihilated, leaving behind a polluted and silent earth.

One had to face this. A third world war was likely; the end of civilization was likely. We believed this strongly in the 1960s. One couldn't run to an outmoded idea of God for comfort. One had to be strong; one had to construct meaning in the silence in the wake of the departure of God.

And so began my journeys through the secular world of America in the 1960s, and so began my flight from the realm of faith and beauty and harmony which had been my childhood. So began my struggles with a harsher discipline than that which I'd left behind.

It is ironic perhaps that I did not subsequently become sexually liberated or wild. Solitary sex relieved the tension I felt, but I remained an extremely conservative well-controlled woman who refused to be intimate with anyone until she found the person with whom she wanted to spend her life.

This was Stan Rice, the boy from high school, who came up to Denton to go to North Texas State College in 1960, and who followed me to San Francisco in 1961. I went back to Denton to marry him in that same year. For all the agony over sex, this was the love of my life. We married as soon as we could because this marriage represented the highest commitment we could make to one another. And we remained married for forty-one years until his death in 2002. I've never been with any other man, but Stan Rice.

So much for sex. So much for all that agony. So much for all that day-in and day-out misery of those crucial years.

There's more to the story in that I later became a nationally famous pornographer for a series of fairytale erotic books written under the pen name A. N. Roquelaure—but that was in the 1980s, and those books contain imaginary characters and imaginary realms.

As for my great desire to read forbidden authors, I was still in my first few years of college severely disabled as a reader, and could only make it through the short stories of Jean-Paul Sartre, and some of the works of Albert Camus. Of the great German philosophers who loomed so large in discussion in those days, I could not read one page.

But I understood Camus' famous *The Myth of Sisyphus* and I understood his concept of "the absurd." I read his novels *The Stranger* and *The Plague*. And I took from these works Camus' urgent faith that we live a moral and responsible life even if nothing is known about how we got here or where we're going, that we make the meaning, that we stand for values which we can't deny.

I got it. It was as rigorous a discipline to believe in the

ideas of Camus as it had ever been to be Catholic. In fact, being an atheist required discipline very like that of being Catholic. One could never yield to the idea of a supernatural authority, no matter how often one might be tempted. To think that a personal God had made the world was to yield to a demonic and superstitious and destructive belief.

Stan Rice, whom I married in 1961, was one of the most conscientious people I'd ever met. He was positively driven by conscience and thought in terms of harsh absolutes. His life was devoted to poetry and, later, to painting; art for him had replaced any religion that he ever had. He scoffed at the idea of a personal God, and scoffed at all religion in general. He did more than scoff. He felt it was stupid, vain, false, and possibly he thought it was evil. I'm not sure on that.

The point for me was that he had intense personal values. And he understood that I wanted to be somebody, and he believed that I should. Though he deplored my sloppiness, lack of discipline, inability to read or study, and general disarray and confusion, he believed in my intellect and in my passions and he found me interesting, more interesting apparently than anyone else.

Never did he question my capacity or my intentions to have a full rich committed life. And I believed of course in his full committed life.

He was a model of personal discipline, a great reader of anything that he chose to read, and a model student, as well as being the most interesting and attractive person that I ever met. He was a great poet, and early on, he became a great reader of his poems before audiences large and small.

We worked our way through college together, and nothing could have shaken our dedication to getting an education or living in a world of ideas and books. Stan's parents had not gone to college and he wanted to be in the college world. I was right with him on this. The fact that we might someday have jobs at a university, that we might make our living in the world of literature, this was our dream.

Part of our marriage was fierce intellectual argument and we often frightened people as we tore at each other, and shouted at each other, and insisted on various abstract points. But in general we had a wonderful time.

I think our marriage was as free of gender inequity as any marriage I knew. It wasn't entirely free, and certainly other people pressured us incessantly to conform to gender-specific roles. If I went on a diet, mutual friends adamantly reminded me that I must still "cook for Stan" so that he got proper meals. People went so far as to say I shouldn't make as good a grade in a class as Stan was making. One male friend furiously insisted that I "admit" Stan was more intelligent than I was. People in the main were far more interested in him than in me, and I existed in his shadow, especially when he began to write and to publicly read his works.

But in general, the jarring remarks of others didn't penetrate the gender equality we maintained. We were both working; we both had dreams. Indeed the preservation of my personal dreams was probably essential to maintaining Stan's admiration, and vice versa.

Stan was an English major, went on to get a graduate degree in English, and went right into teaching at San Francisco State, our alma mater, and was soon put on tenure track, on the strength of his abilities as a teacher, and his poetry which commanded terrific respect. It was highly exceptional for a graduate of San Francisco State to be accepted there as a full-time teacher, especially if one did not have a Ph.D., but Stan was accepted and he became one of the youngest professors on the faculty, and he continued to teach at San Francisco State until 1988.

I had a much more difficult time. I couldn't keep up in English classes. It was the reading problem. When an English teacher told us to read a play by Shakespeare in a week, I knew that this was virtually impossible for me and I dropped out of English and started wandering, simply seeking a liberal arts education, and ending up as a political science major because classes in political science were understandable to me on the basis of lectures, as well as on the basis of some reading, and I was able to do well in this field. I graduated with a B.A. in political science after five years, and together with Stan who graduated summa cum laude in English after four years.

We both went on to graduate school. And in graduate school I did finally learn to read. The world of literature was gradually opened to me, and certainly the world of history was opened, and I was seldom without a book at my side after those times.

It's pointless to describe my whole life as an atheist, or to attempt a personal memoir here of how I became a published writer.

What matters for the sake of this memoir is that I learned in college all I could possibly contain about the modern world. My learning was disorderly, haphazard, at times daring, obsessive, and full of gaps and blind spots. But I sought freely the answers to my questions.

And the principal moral lessons I learned had to do with the Great Wars.

I'd been four years old when the United States dropped the atom bomb on Hiroshima. I learned in college that this had happened. It was a profound shock. It was in college that I learned about the Holocaust, from films like *The Pawnbroker* with Rod Steiger, and from documentaries in the theater and on television. It was in college that I read (slowly) *All Quiet on the Western Front.*

Our professors had fought in the Second World War or experienced the war firsthand in some way. They sought to make us understand what this war had meant for Europe and for the world. And I remember impassioned lectures on the terrible Great War of attrition that had preceded the Second World War, and what that first war had "done to rational Europe," to all its hopes and dreams.

This was something I wanted desperately to grasp.

Again, the primary source of education here was lectures, not books. Remarque's novel, Hemingway's novels, other fiction, gave me something of the experience and impact of these wars, but the professors really established the context, the seriousness of what had happened, and directed the reading I chose. I gravitated to brilliant lecturers, men and women who could give me a coherent picture of the world. And all of my radiant memories have to do with lectures, or moments during lectures when certain immense ideas became clear.

I don't know what anybody else heard in those classrooms, but I was seeking to understand things like why the color and figure went out of art after the Impressionists, and why artists like Picasso, with his wild, brutal abstractions, rose to the fore. I sought to understand all of history, actually, dipping back into the centuries as I took art classes, and dreaming of traveling to places to which we couldn't afford to go.

I longed for a coherent theory of history that was beyond my grasp.

As for what was going on around me—the feminist movement, the rise of the hippies, the transformation of the Haight-Ashbury of San Francisco (where I happened to live), the Vietnam War protests—I ignored these things pretty much. They didn't interest me, per se. I had no perspective on the emancipation of women or how key it was to the conditions of my own daily life. I couldn't see how rapidly it was advancing. I think I ignored militant feminism because it was too painful for me to become involved in the fray.

Also there was no way that a young person like me, with such limited mental tools, could grasp that we were in fact experiencing one of the most tumultuous and significant times in world history.

I had no sense then that I'd been born into a world of rampant social experiment, and I did not see the world-transforming significance of the emancipation of women, and the liberation of gays.

I was too focused on the past.

As for the civil rights movement, I missed it. I'd left the South before it started; and I was in California almost the entire time that the key court decisions were made. Thousands of young people were being radicalized by their participation in this movement. I wasn't aware of it. I was deep into my timeless studies, often experiencing profound insights into social situations for which I had little or no continuous context.

But I'm not sure many other people struggling through the 1960s and 1970s realized how unique were the changes that we saw.

Assumptions about race and gender were being thrown out the window.

The Western family was being entirely reconfigured. Women had attained more legal rights and privileges in ten years than they had in seven thousand years before. Respectable men and women lived together out of wedlock. No-fault divorce came into existence. Contraceptive devices and drugs were readily available. The prosecution of rape as a crime underwent a transformation, in which the victim was no longer on trial, but the perpetrator.

The Vietnam War polarized the country. Illegal drugs spread from the campus elites to the middle classes and to the working classes, and ultimately to the criminal classes. Millions of women not only had access to more jobs than ever before, but discovered they had to work for a living, whether they wanted to or not, and the "stay-at-home wife" became a rare being, along with the husband willing to support her.

All this was simply too vast, too swift, too inexorable for people to comprehend. Social and economic forces were too intermingled with the voices of protest or the prophets of social justice. I saw life transformed for millions of Americans, out of the corner of my eye.

Meantime, my early years in San Francisco were rich years. Foreign films were the rage, which meant continued exposure to the work of Ingmar Bergman, Federico Fellini, Antonioni, Buñuel, and Truffaut. San Francisco has marvelous small theaters in which we saw the plays of Sartre and Camus. All this educated me in ways that books could not.

And around me, as ever, were good people, conscientious people, secular people who on principle wanted to make our world a better world—for the black person, for the woman, for the poor. I can't emphasize this enough: in San Francisco and later in Berkeley, I saw secular humanism as something beautiful and vigorous and brave. And looking back on it, I still see it in that way.

The great hippie revolution occurred as I was finishing my undergraduate years, and I found myself in the thick of it, living as we did one-half block off Haight Street in an apartment house that came to include the famous Free Clinic of the neighborhood.

Friends and relatives trooped through our apartment, marveling at the paintings on the walls, at Stan's poems hanging over his typewriter, at our intense and high-pitched intellectual life amid piles of books and sometime domestic confusion, a world in which Stan and I pounded away on our separate typewriters or argued furiously about philosophy and literature, no matter who might be there to witness the screaming and get upset.

People all around us were discussing the ideas of Timothy Leary, the effects of LSD, the joy of being a dropout artist. Marijuana smoke was thick in the air. It was the incense of the church of psychedelic transformation. People took carefully structured LSD trips with others who had experienced the drug, acting as protective "guides."

I was no more part of this than I had been part of childhood or adolescence. I was working at a fairly high-paying job in a theater box office downtown as I went to school. I showed up for art class in high heels and stockings, no matter who said what, and ignored the pressure of my hippie friends to leave "the establishment" or drop out of school.

I didn't touch LSD. I was too afraid that it would drive me out of my mind. And the new revolutionaries provided me with a whole series of new gender shocks.

In the midst of rampant liberation, the flower children were stridently if not viciously sexist. "Chicks" were supposed to bake bread, clean up, feed their hippie boyfriends, and if at all possible hold a job to support the artist-poets of the group, and perhaps even fork over a bit of financial support received from frantic parents back home. It was no accident that these "chicks" wore long dresses and long hair. They looked like pioneer women, and they worked just about that hard. There was so much pejorative talk of "chicks not knowing how to be chicks," and how "chicks" were anti-marijuana, and how "chicks" were middle class, and how if your "old lady" was a real "old lady," she should feed you, and how "chicks" brought you down nagging at you to do chores and things, or make a living, that I withdrew from the company around me in alienation and disgust.

But all this was superficial compared to the real changes in the status of women and gay people that were taking place. This was nothing. But it was the nothing that surrounded me and threatened me, and the nothing from which I withdrew.

As we rolled into the 1970s, I continued naturally and unconsciously to ignore anyone who ever sought to define me as a woman, because I didn't feel like one, and I made the tragic mistake of saying casually, "I don't like women," which I would never do now. I wanted to separate myself from a class of beings who were being treated essentially like dirt, at the very moment in history that they were gaining unprecedented freedom and rights.

I couldn't see the larger picture. I didn't understand feminism in a fair or reasonable way. I was fleeing from being a woman; and feminism invited too much pain.

I was in graduate school when my daughter became sick. Two years later, after her death before her sixth birthday, I became a writer.

It was practically an accident, and yet it was the most deliberate thing I ever did. The book was *Interview with the Vampire.*

I recognize now that it was distinctly postmodern in its use of nineteenth-century characters, opulent sets, and ornamented, adjective-laden prose. It was distinctly postmodern in its use of old-fashioned plot and straightforward narrative, and in its use of heroic characters. Modernism had supposedly killed the well-plotted novel. It had supposedly killed the hero. Well, not for me. I didn't even really know what modernism was.

The novel was also an obvious lament for my lost faith.

The vampires roam in a world without God; and Louis, the heartbroken hero, searches for a meaningful context in vain.

But for the purposes of this narrative, what is also important is that the book was a flight from gender, a flight from the world of which I couldn't make any sense.

In my fiction, the characters were practically androgynes. The vampire heroes, Louis and Lestat, had feminine beauty, luxuriant hair, rich velvet clothes, and preternatural strength. They loved each other or others, with no regard for gender, and they loved the child vampire Claudia in a way that established a polymorphous sensuality for the entire work. The work wasn't about literal sex. The work was about the "marriage of true minds" beyond impediments. The work had nothing to do with domestic struggle, or class struggle, or gender struggle. The work transcended all of this. The work was about my own fierce polymorphous view of the world in which an old woman might be as beautiful as a young male child. My book reflected a fusion of the aesthetic and the moral with some tentative connection to the lost harmony of my Catholic girlhood.

Where did such a view come from? How had it been sustained?

This book established me as a writer. And to a large extent, the sexism I took for granted in the behavior of others dropped away overnight. There were still people around who reminded me "to take care of" my husband's ego, or inquired tactlessly and in the presence of others as to how Stan was "taking all this." There were even people who came to Stan to request funds for various projects, laying out their demands to him, in front of me, as if I did not exist.

But this was not significant.

In the main, I ceased to be somebody's wife. I became the author Anne Rice, and generally when people spoke to me, they had something to say to me and it was about my work. And that meant it was about my mind—this genderless and oversensuous mind.

I didn't realize this immediately. I've never realized anything immediately in my life. But in truth, my life had changed.

I was that *person* now in the eyes of the world that I had always been in my own eyes. *Personhood had come at last.* The goal of my life had been attained.

Another dramatic event transformed my life at this time and, very possibly, saved it. I gave birth to a healthy and beautiful son, Christopher, on March 11, 1978. Stan and I were elated. But within less than a year, we became painfully conscious of our heavy drinking, and the impact this was having on our care for our son. Neither of us wanted this priceless child to grow up in a household with two drunken parents. On Memorial Day of 1979, we made a pact never to drink again, and though I violated the pact that summer, when I went home to New Orleans for the funeral of an uncle, I took my last drink the night before flying back to California.

If Christopher had not come to us at that time, it is very likely that heavy drinking would have killed Stan and me, or so diminished our existence and our capacity to work that we would have experienced a slow and ugly disintegration.

We'd confronted this possibility many a time. But our resolves to stop drinking had never been lasting. The love of Christopher, and our hopes and dreams for him, now provided the incentive we needed. Though we did not join any organization or 12-step program, we maintained sobriety from then on.

As I look back on it, I think that Christopher was aptly named, because he brought a saving grace into our lives that was all but miraculous. A child of exceptional gifts, he surprised us, challenged us, and educated us over the years in countless ways, as only a child can do, and he is now a highly successful novelist. He was and is a treasure. And he was as much a part of my life from then on as any success I derived from my writing.

We were a trio, Stan and Christopher and I, as our existence underwent remarkable changes.

I wrote twenty-one books before faith returned to me. And in almost all these books, creatures shut out of life, doomed to marginality or darkness, seek for lives of value, even when the world tells them they cannot have such lives. In all of these works, gender doesn't matter. What matters is the personality of the individual, and his or her desires. Historical settings are of huge importance, and they are used much like the speculative settings of science fiction writers, to establish a matrix in which ideas can be tested and explored, to establish a laboratory in which experiments in loving and suffering and persevering can be completed with success.

Of course the historical research for my books drew me into periods of history that I deeply loved; this was natural to me, to research eighteenth-century Venice, or Renaissance Florence. I was in full control of characters both masculine and feminine. I was both.

And the historical research for my novels became one of

my greatest passions, and certainly the new source of education, as I had long left college behind.

I wrote by instinct.

I poured out the darkness and despair of an atheist struggling to establish bonds and hopes in a godless world where anything might, and could, happen, where happiness could be torn away from one in an instant, a world in which the condemned and the despised raised their voices in protest and song.

Over and over I wrote about outcasts—young people of color in pre–Civil War New Orleans who could not be fully part of white society; castrati opera singers in eighteenth-century Italy, who could not marry under the laws of the lands in which they became superstars adored by all; vampires who could not endure the light of the sun and were doomed to fall in love with the beauty and sanctity of the human lives they destroyed. I wrote about witches—psychic humans with the capacity to attract supernatural forces that seem to obey no laws of right and wrong. I wrote about the Jews of ancient Babylon, struggling to maintain their autonomy as a people "in a strange land."

Very few of my characters were females.

When I did write about a feminine protagonist, I sensed a different response to the plot and to the character on the part of critics. Love scenes involving males were treated with dignity. A book involving a man and woman was dismissed as "a cheap romance." I took careful note of this. I came to avoid using women except in ways that wouldn't invite this dismissal. Still it happened. I don't say this lightly. Critics had it "in" for the female characters I created in a way that they never had it "in" for the males.

This is still the case.

Readers reflected this somewhat as well. They might adore a melancholy hero like the vampire Louis, or fall in love with the passionate and irrepressible vampire Lestat. But they were offended by the vampire Pandora, and put off by the young Mona Mayfair, who was in her own way no less interesting than the male characters in the book. The heroine of my novel *Belinda* was actually criticized for not being a typical teenager! And this from readers who had accepted a fourteen-year-old male Creole genius or tragic young vampires cursing Heaven with raised fists. Lestat's boasts were received as charming. Mona was viewed as impertinent. Belinda was ignored because she was not a stereotype.

In sum, if I created a woman the way I wanted that woman to be, for many people this didn't work. My female characters were measured in terms of gender. With male characters I could achieve just about anything I wanted to achieve. Male characters didn't really have any gender. Female characters were cursed and confined by it in the minds of those who read the books.

I can't say I reacted literally to this experience. I was aware of it; it influenced me subconsciously or consciously in fragmented form. I did not set out to do anything about it. But it had its inevitable effect.

But by and large, I wrote what I felt impelled to write. I was the "he" of my fiction. Or the "she" of it in those few times when a woman entered the scene.

Perhaps the most significant book I wrote before my conversion to Christianity was the novel *Violin*. There are many complex reasons why this book was important to me, why it involved pain and exposure that some of the other books did not. But I am convinced to this day that the reason my readers largely overlooked it was the fact that it involves a woman's creative experience and not that of a man. If a gorgeous gay man had taken the place in the book of Triana Becker, the public response might have had considerably more depth. Whatever the case, the book is not only about grief and faith, and the redemptive potential of art—this it has in common with all my books—but it is also about my childhood, about the chapel in New Orleans where I first experienced faith in God. It's about the losses I suffered as a child, and about my core beliefs regarding art and blood—metaphoric blood and literal blood. It is perhaps the cleanest allegory of my own creative life. However, allegories of my own creative life fill my other books, including most especially *The Vampire Armand* and the novel *Blood and Gold*.

Why I managed to become such a financial success at all is a bit of a mystery. These books were each eccentric, one differing violently from the one before it, and the entire oeuvre made almost no concessions to the marketplace at all. True there is plot, character, spectacle, and tragedy in these books, but the books are not easy to read, and they are too eccentric to be easily described. The only people who provide easy descriptions of them are people who have never read them. Because these books involve the supernatural, they are apparently extremely easy to condemn or dismiss.

But success I enjoyed, no matter what turn in the road I took.

Let me suggest one reason why the books found a mass audience. They were written by someone whose auditory and visual experiences shaped the prose. As I've mentioned over and over in this book, I am a terrible reader. But my mind is filled with these auditory and visual lessons and, powered by them, I can write about five times faster than I can read.

Somehow this led to my developing a style which sought to make real for the reader the acoustic and iconic world in which I'd been formed as a child. Almost all of my key learning had been imprinted on the right side of my brain.

Drawing on the left side of my brain, apparently, I used words to go beyond words.

Also because I wasn't "literary" by nature, I looked to old-fashioned models in my writing. I've mentioned this above. I didn't "get" modernism. I didn't "get" pedestrian realism, the values of which essentially controlled "high literature" of the 1970s, 1980s, and 1990s. I didn't care about pedestrian realism or ordinary people. Mediocrity meant nothing to me, and a literature devoted to anatomizing mediocre or "typical" people was uninviting to me. In fact, it was almost impenetrable to me.

I wanted to tell stories of great lifetimes, of spiritual quests, and of tragic adolescent discovery, and of great moral battles between great individual souls and the social world. These aren't what anyone would call contemporary themes.

I also wrote passionately about characters whom I personally loved. I was never interested in exposing or destroying or punishing characters. I never became obsessed by those whom I did not like. So my writing lacked irony and cynicism, and it lacked sarcasm.

And in this I was not modern but appealed rather to an audience that wanted to be swept up in the spiritual journey of a hero rather than proceed through the cooler pages of the fiction of alienation and cleverness. My work isn't critical of society, nor does it affirm nothingness. It's romantic in the full old-fashioned sense of the word. It can be seen as naïve. And certainly it can be dismissed as sentimental.

As already mentioned, I also believed intensely in spectacle—flamboyant behavior, violent clashes, a certain swashbuckling type of action which I'd learned from radio and from the films of the fifties that had made such a strong mark on my nonliterate mind. In my work, I strove for the high-pitched beauty of Michael Powell's *The Tales of Hoffmann* or *The Red Shoes*.

That there was an audience for this warmer approach to fiction isn't surprising. The high literary pedestrian realism of the 1970s tended to scorn the "mass audience." I didn't scorn the mass audience. I was part of it. In fact, I embraced the mass audience with a certain recklessness that often elicited from intellectuals a blatant contempt.

Countless times people out of the mass audience have come up to me and said, "Yours are the only books I can read." Others have said, "Yours are the only novels I've *ever* read." Still others have said, "Your novels started me reading. After I read you, I read everything. But before that I never read at all."

Of course the novels, like any novels, are only fully accessible to those who can in fact read them, can in fact be swept along by the decided rhythm of the sentences, and those who can respond to the choice of adjectives as well as the choice of concrete nouns.

But concrete nouns and action verbs actually underpin all my writing. And there is always urgency, a driving pace. There is, as mentioned above, a beginning and middle, and also an end, though often the end refuses to be an end in the artificial sense and makes the reader furious. In other words, the novels for all their strangeness usually have a conventional feel to them in terms of story, a feel somewhat like that of Dickens or Brontë, the first writing teachers I ever had.

As for the revolt against modernism, my writing doesn't in fact reflect the war on modernism that was part of my earlier Catholic world. The books are too transgressive, they're too committed to sexual freedom and gender equality to be part of that old Catholic war. They reflect, rather, the changing contemporary world which I pretty much ignored. The appeal is for the equality of persons, and for the redemption of sexuality as something which is not inherently sinful or sin related.

The books do protest the severity of modern architecture and painting, and the dissonance of modern music.

They go back into the baroque, the rococo, and the Romantic, but they take with them decidedly optimistic visions of sexuality and the supremacy of art.

They refuse to be classified as any one type of writing.

They attract all sorts of readers, and there is no consensus among even the most ardent fans of the books as to what the books mean.

Every time one of the books is adapted in film or onstage or for television, there is a huge disagreement amongst the people involved as to what the book is about. And there is a subsequent controversy among the members of the audience as to what the books are about.

Throughout the years that I created these books one by one, some during periods of hypomanic happiness, others during periods of black despair, I paid little or no attention to these controversies except to now and then become hysterical and angry in my declarations as to what the books were trying to do. Lot of good that did.

Oftentimes what interested me in a particular book went entirely unnoticed by the readers talking to me about it, or writing about it. And certainly most of the newspaper and magazine reviews had little or nothing to do with my ambitions or whatever I might have achieved.

One could write a book about all this. Perhaps I will in the future. Right now I prefer not even to write a chapter.

What matters here is this:

These books transparently reflect a journey through atheism and back to God. It is impossible not to see this. They reflect an attempt to determine what is good and what is evil in an atheistic world. They are about the struggle of brothers and sisters in a world without credible fathers and mothers. They reflect an obsession with the possibility of a new and enlightened moral order.

Did I know this when I wrote them? No.

But the research I did for them, the digging through history, the studying of ancient history in particular, was actually laying the ground for my return to faith.

The more I read of history—any history—the more my atheism became shaky. History, as well as Creation, was talking to me about God. The great personalities of history were talking to me about God.

In particular, the survival of the Jews, which I had studied so keenly for the novels *Servant of the Bones,* and *Pandora,* and *Blood and Gold,* was talking to me about God. I was seeing patterns in history that I could not account for according to the theories of history I'd inherited in school. I was seeing something in the survival of the Jews in particular for which there was no convincing sociological or economic explanation at all.

A great love of the Jewish people began to burn in me, a love of this tribe that had survived since the most ancient times into the present day. I conceived a fierce curiosity about them, and everything pertaining to them. I was drawn to them in their piety and integrity. And I wanted to know how Christianity had arisen from their religion, and how, above all, had it managed to take the Western world by storm.

If any one "thing" in all my studies led me back to Christ, it was His people, the Jews.

Now I had grown up knowing nobody who was Jewish, until a certain time in my early teens when an Orthodox Jewish family rented a flat at the end of our block. Our house faced St. Charles Avenue; their house faced Carondelet. How we became aware of them, I don't recall. I remember the father of the family singing in Hebrew, and my mother remarking that he was a cantor. She listened to him and drew my attention to listening to him, with palpable delight. She spoke of him and his family with a certain reverence.

At that time I was a member of the Legion of Mary, and part of what we did in that Catholic group was good deeds. I took it upon myself to babysit for the brilliant children of this Orthodox Jewish family when the parents went to the synagogue, or even out on the town. This was a good deed I did for no pay. The children included a brilliant boy named Benjamin and a brilliant girl named Clara. These children spoke probably more than three languages. I didn't know where they had come from but they told horrific stories of war—of houses wrecked, of rats jumping into cradles, of hardship beyond anything I'd ever personally heard described. They were cheerful and brilliant; the parents did not speak English and we communicated by gesture and sign. The cantor had a black beard and he wore a yarmulke, and his singing had an unearthly beauty to it that I loved.

It was a tragedy to me when this family moved away.

My last night at their house was spent sitting in the doorway guarding it, as they were in the process of moving, and I spent this evening in conversation with a young man who knew the family, an immensely attractive and mysterious person who always wore a hat. I recall speaking of spiritual things with him, of my desire to be a nun. He expressed admiration for women who gave their lives to their religion. I explained that we weren't giving our lives to our religion, we were giving them to God. He showed a respect for this.

Indeed his entire manner was serious and agreeable. He explained to me why the family I so loved was moving to New York. "There are not many people like them here," he said, "but there are a lot of people like them in New York." I was happy for them, but I missed them. I never forgot them. I wonder today what became of Clara and Benjamin, and the baby in the crib whose name I don't recall.

Let's come back to 1998. I'm in New Orleans. I'm a successful writer. I'm thinking all the time about the Jews, about how much in common that family had with the Jews of history, the Jews emerging from the pages of the history books I'm reading about ancient times.

Of course by this time I'd had innumerable Jewish friends, and of all my close friends, they had been the most spiritual and the most intellectually passionate. Though secular people in the main, they retained a theological way of looking at life, a deep moral pressure to do "what was right." They were highly artistic, and artistic principles were mixed in with their fervent attitude towards life. They seemed to have a vision of life that was religious, and at times even mystical, in that they believed in a value to art and good behavior which could not necessarily be justified by social custom.

What had my experience with Catholicism been up to this time? Just about nil.

For just about thirty years, I'd suffered such an aversion to Catholicism that I avoided any mention of it anywhere, including any sustained contact with anyone who was Catholic. I'd heard rumblings of big changes in the Catholic Church, horror stories of the loss of the Latin liturgy, of an English Mass. I'd heard that the great church council Vatican II was responsible for this artistic disaster. I'd heard that thousands of priests and nuns had left the church.

But I didn't really know what was happening in contemporary Catholicism any more than I'd known the latest church history in 1960.

In fact, during all these years away from the church, there had been only one film about Catholicism that I had watched over and over again.

This was a film that I deeply and painfully loved. It was called *The Nun's Story* and it was made in 1959. It starred Audrey Hepburn in an exceptional and subdued performance as a Catholic woman in Belgium who enters a semi-cloistered order of nuns in the hopes of becoming a missionary in the Belgian Congo. It is an austere and pure film to an exceptional degree.

It is entirely about the inner spiritual struggle of this one person, and her failure to become the religious she had hoped to become. It is devoid of cheap romance, or distracting subplots that might have appealed to a commercial audience. In fact, it is such a pure film that it is almost impossible to understand how it ever got made. But it did get made, and time and again, I watched it, sometimes crying, grieving for my lost Catholic faith.

I felt I understood the struggle of Sister Luke in this film completely.

She was guilty of the sin we had imputed to Martin Luther. Because she could not be perfect according to the system, she left the system. In Luther's case it had been the church. In Sister Luke's case, it was the convent. Her tragedy was entirely a spiritual tragedy, and I never watched this film without realizing that it could have been my own story, and that perhaps it should have been my own story, that I should have tried to be a nun as I had once dreamed of doing. I loved everything about this film. I loved the shots of the convent with its broad corridors and high doors. I loved the soft, dignified grace of Sister Luke as she accepted the penance of wearing the ornate habit of her order. I loved that she cared above all about being a good person with her entire heart. I loved even perhaps that she failed, failed as I had failed. She'd left the convent. I'd left God.

I should point out that this film is genderless. The story could easily have been about a monk. In being about a religious person, it transcends gender obsessions and concerns completely, and that is no doubt the reason that it spoke so purely to me about faith, about the love of God, and about the kind of life that is possible when one offers everything to God.

In 1974, I actually read the book on which the film was based. I found that the film had been true to the book. And Sister Luke's story was my way of visiting my old church, my magnificent and timeless church, and being there, in sorrow, for a little while. The story was set in World War II. That was long before the great church council of Vatican II which supposedly changed my church, and so I felt a special refuge in the film. It was the way things had been, and perhaps were not, for anyone, anymore.

In 1998, I actually didn't know how things were in the Catholic Church. I had no idea at all.

Now for ten years, I'd been living in New Orleans. Stan and Christopher and I had come there to live in 1988. And one most significant development in those years had been the complete acceptance of us by our huge extended Catholic family, including the revered Murphy cousins whom I mentioned early in this book.

In 1988, my father had been still living, and he'd come to join me in New Orleans, and there amid huge family parties he had connected me with his surviving brothers and sisters, and aunts and uncles, and all the cousins he so cherished and loved. This was my father's last great gift to me—that he brought me into contact with this "lost" family. And my father's happiness at this time was also a gift.

To my amazement, these churchgoing people completely embraced Stan and Christopher and me. They didn't question my disconnection from Catholicism. They said nothing about the transgressive books I'd written. They simply welcomed us into their homes and into their arms.

This was as shocking as it was wonderful. The Catholics of my time had been bound to shun people who left the faith. Indeed one reason I stayed clear of all Catholics for three decades was that I expected to be rejected and shunned.

In my childhood, one couldn't enter a non-Catholic church. If a cousin married "out of the church," not only must one shun the ceremony, one had to shun the cousin forever after. An entire branch of our family had been lost to us in the 1950s because they became Protestants. So, returning to New Orleans, I more or less expected to be shunned.

But the world of my Catholic cousins in New Orleans was a loving world. And these were indeed people who went to

CALLED OUT OF DARKNESS

Mass and Communion on Sunday, who participated in their church, who visibly and actively supported it. These were the ones who had stayed.

This acceptance puzzled me and interested me. How could they be Catholics and put their arms around a woman who wrote *Interview with the Vampire*? How could they come into my home so cheerfully when they knew Stan and I were not married "in the church"? Surely they knew Christopher was being brought up with no religious affiliation. True, he went to Trinity Episcopal School, but that was because Trinity was a fine school.

I never asked them these questions. I felt an overwhelming love for them, and my return to New Orleans became a return to their acceptance as much as a return to the church buildings and the venerable houses I so loved.

As I met more and more churchgoing friends, I was intrigued by the way they managed to live in the world as Catholics. Again, I asked no questions. I simply observed.

No harsh mental break had ever forced itself upon these people. They had found a way to live faithfully with absolutes, and above all they had found a way to continue day in and day out believing in God.

When my great-aunt, Sister Mary Liguori, died, my eleven-year-old son, Christopher, was a pallbearer at her funeral. We stood with all the other Catholic mourners, and from memory, I followed the prayers. Of course I believed that I could never really be one of these people again. I couldn't believe in God!

But the simple fact was: I did. The world of atheism was cracking apart for me, just as once the world of Catholic faith had cracked apart. I was losing my faith in the nonexistence of God.

I was, however, being doggedly and religiously faithful to an atheism in which I no longer believed. There was a fatalism to it. *You can't go back to God! Why do you dream of this? You know too much, you've seen too much, you just can't accept all the social things these people obviously believe. Besides, you know there is no God. The world's meaningless. People have to provide the meaning. You've been writing about this for thirty years!*

At some point I began to contribute to the local church—the parish church of my childhood—though I never set foot inside. Through that support I became friends with the local Redemptorist Fathers, one of whom was my cousin, though I wasn't a member of the faith.

As I've described, I have a deep devotion to the Redemptorist Fathers. I had never forgotten that my father's seminary education had set him apart from his sisters and brothers, and given him a love of literature and music as well as a spiritual intensity that few around him possessed.

I also became a great collector of religious artifacts, of the life-size statues of the saints that were falling into the hands of antique dealers as old inner-city churches closed across the United States.

I had a perfect place to put all this art. It was a building called St. Elizabeth's Orphanage which I had bought from the Daughters of Charity in the mid-1990s—a vast brick building built between the 1860s and the 1880s that bore a heartbreaking resemblance to the old home of the Little Sisters of the Poor in which I'd wanted so much to be a nun some forty years before.

What was I doing when I bought that building? I lovingly restored its chapel. I bought any plaster saint or virgin or angel anyone offered me. I even discovered, in a French Quarter antique shop, a whole set of the Stations of the Cross which had once hung in St. Alphonsus Church, my very church, and I bought them and ranged them up the main staircase. Yet another ornate set, offered by a country priest, was bought, restored, and ranged along the chapel walls.

In addition to the beautiful Garden District home I'd acquired soon after my arrival, I bought the very house on St. Charles Avenue where our family had lived for a short while before my mother's death. This house had once belonged to the Redemptorist church parish. We'd rented it from them for a short while. It had been before that a priest house, and before that the convent of the Mercy Sisters. It was adjacent to the mansion on Prytania Street that held the Our Mother of Perpetual Help Chapel where I'd first prayed to God. I bought that building too.

Think of it. Think of buying the building in which you first went to pray, the building that contained your mother's old high school classrooms, the building that contained the chapel in which your mother's Requiem Mass had been said. From that chapel, my mother's remains had been taken to the graveyard.

I guess I would have bought the graveyard if it had been for sale, as well.

Bit by bit I was picking up the pieces of a Catholic childhood with these significant purchases. I was forming alliances with those still within the fold. I was keeping company with their loving kindness and their daily faith. Yet every step was marked with pessimism, sadness, and a grief on the edge of despair. Every step was marked by darkness—by a tragic certainty that belief in God Himself was quite beyond my conscience and my heart. There was no returning to any church without faith in God.

Beyond the matrix of gilded plaster, stone, and image, there loomed the threat—the ominous and dreadful threat—of the love of Almighty God.

> *Still with unhurrying chase,*
> *And unperturbed pace,*
> *Deliberate speed, majestic instancy,*
> *Came on the following Feet,*
> *And a Voice above their beat—*
> *"Naught shelters thee, who wilt not shelter Me."*
>
> —Francis Thompson,
> "The Hound of Heaven"

7

BEFORE I MOVE ON to the actual moment that my faith came back to me, let me say a few words about pilgrimages, because by the 1990s, I was making them all the time.

Emotional lives have landscapes. Interior journeys have an exterior geography. The geography of my life has always been intense and dramatic. I knew this when I was growing up.

St. Charles Avenue was a great historic artery of New Orleans. On the far side of that street, the Garden District began, enclosing the finest and most significant antebellum houses in the city, outside of the French Quarter downtown. That I had to walk from St. Charles Avenue, through that eerie and enchanting neighborhood, in order to get to the Irish Channel and its two enormous churches was significant. I passed from a world of wealth and charm into a world of work and economy, yet the journey ended in a vast

Romanesque church, St. Alphonsus, which is even now a jaw-dropping wonder to those who visit it.

My later writing always sought to recapture the harmony, the lushness, and the timeless loveliness of the Garden District, whether I was writing literally about the neighborhood itself, or about Venice, or Vienna, or Haiti, or Rome.

And my novels always sought to express the intensity and the high-pitched allegory and symbol of the church.

The noisy and narrow streets of the Irish Channel were the map of the world that I feared—the world without art, the world without timeless beauty, the world of necessity and raw experience, and random suffering, into which anyone at any time might suddenly drop, the world in which someone by circumstance might be completely trapped.

I didn't grow up in the Garden District. I didn't grow up in the Irish Channel. I grew up on the margins of the world that included both.

I don't belong anywhere. I don't come from any particular milieu. No group embraced my eccentric family. My mother's dreams of raising four perfectly healthy children and four geniuses probably died with her. Her death was a catastrophe. She was forty-eight and beautiful. She was brilliant, perhaps the most brilliant person I've ever known. She died of the drink. We didn't save her.

By the time I came home to buy a mansion in the Garden District, indeed to buy the very house in which she had been living when she died, well, she had been gone for over thirty years.

But I get ahead of my story.

Let me drop back.

Geography is important.

At the beginning of my career as a novelist, I began to seek God in geography rather consciously though with no expressed hope of ever finding Him in the journeys and pilgrimages I made.

As soon as the money flowed in from *Interview with the Vampire,* Stan and I went to Europe. What interested me above all were churches. The Cathedral of Chartres and Notre Dame de Paris were what I wanted to see in France. The Louvre, the Jeu de Paume, those were extra experiences, wonderful though they were.

In Rome, it was St. Peter's that drew me, and then all the other magnificent churches of the Eternal City, as well as the Vatican Museum and the Sistine Chapel.

Within a year of that first trip to Europe, I went back to Italy with my father and stepmother and younger sister. We journeyed to Rome, Florence, and Venice. And we also went to Assisi, where I stood in a long line of pilgrims, waiting for a few moments to press my hands to the tomb of St. Francis, whom I'd loved so much as a child.

Again, I found myself wandering through St. Peter's Basilica, gazing on the crypts of popes, and on the wondrously colored marble work, and staring at the varied monuments of my ancient Catholic faith.

In the town of Siena, it was the cathedral that drew me. In Venice, I sat in San Marco staring at the walls of tessellated gold.

Art, yes, art, that's what I was seeking, but what else was I looking for as I wandered silent—refusing to pray, refusing to believe in God—through all those houses of worship? I told myself I was grieving for St. Francis, grieving for the church, grieving for belief which was inaccessible and unrecoverable.

The journey went on.

As mentioned above, I had returned to New Orleans with Stan and with our son, Christopher (note the name), in 1988, and I moved right back into the Redemptorist parish in which I'd been brought up. I moved onto the very block where my Murphy cousins, the Catholic exemplars of our childhood, still maintained their family home.

As already mentioned, I soon purchased the dream houses of my childhood, the huge pre–Civil War Greek Revival "mansions" that had been completely beyond my family's wildest dreams.

Okay. This was a key part of my search for home, for mother, for lost faith.

Other geography underlies the journey as well.

In the mid-1990s I decided, against the advice and inclinations of everyone else, to go to Israel. I wanted to see the Holy Land. I told myself no faith in God was driving me there. I wanted only to see the geography which had meant so much to other people's faith. I was secretly obsessed with Jesus Christ, but I didn't tell anyone, and I didn't tell myself.

Stan went with me along with two devoted assistants, and for a little over a week, we wandered all over Jerusalem, through its most famous and wonderful churches, we visited Nazareth and we visited Bethlehem, and we stood before ancient altars, and in ancient crypts, and wandered ancient terrain.

What was I looking for? Why did I insist that we remain in the church at the Garden of Gethsemane, as three priests said the Mass in three different languages all at the same time? What did it mean to me to be staring at the Garden of Olives where just possibly Our Lord and Savior experienced His agony before Judas and the soldiers came to make the arrest that changed the history of the world?

During those years, I began to collect books on Jesus, and there were a great many being published. The "historical Jesus" was a hot topic in the 1990s. I picked up books wherever I saw them, and simply put them on my shelves to read at some later time. My publisher sent me Paula Fredriksen's *Jesus of Nazareth*. I took the time to read it and was fascinated by it.

I continued to deny faith in God. I truly didn't think faith was possible again for me. Atheism was reality, and one could not turn away from that reality into a cowardly embrace of religion which one knew to be false. I was just "interested in Jesus," because Jesus was an extremely interesting man.

I determined to go to Brazil. At some time in my childhood I'd seen in a film the harbor of Rio de Janeiro; and what I most vividly associated with the harbor was the great statue of Jesus Christ with His arms outstretched that rises from the summit of the mountain in the middle of the city. I'd always wanted to go to that spot.

Again, I told myself I believed in nothing. I was fulfilling childhood fantasies. I was looking for adventure. I was, as a writer and a traveler, living the life I'd dreamed of as a child.

But the compulsion to go to Rio was overwhelming, and we soon made the climb up Corcovado to the foot of the statue of Our Lord.

We took the tram up the steep mountain, which is some 710 meters in height. Then we made the final ascent on foot with hundreds of other tourists, stage by stage, until we reached the statue's base.

The statue is concrete and is 38 meters tall. That means it's about one hundred feet high. It weighs 1,145 tons. As we approached the base of it, the soaring figure was covered completely in clouds.

Imagine, if you can, how enormous this statue was, how inherently impressive, and what it was like to stand at the foot of it, with all of Rio spreading out beyond the stone balustrades of the cliff. Clouds formed and fragmented and came together again over the city of Rio.

I had the feeling we were at the top of the world.

Suddenly the clouds broke, revealing the giant figure of Jesus Christ above us, with His outstretched arms.

The moment was beyond any rational description. It didn't matter to me what anyone else felt or wanted from this journey. I had come thousands of miles to stand here. And here was the Lord.

The clouds quickly closed over the statue; then broke and revealed the statue again. How many times this happened I don't remember. I do remember a kind of delirium, a kind of joy. I'd made it to Rio, I'd made it to the statue of legend, and the physical world contrived to render the moment infinitely more beautiful than I'd imagined it would be.

I didn't acknowledge faith in these moments at the foot of the statue. But something greater than a creedal formulation took hold of me, a sense that this Lord of Lords belonged to me in all His beauty and grandeur. He belonged to me in the grandeur of this symbol if He did not belong to me in any other way.

There was a sadness to this happiness, an undercurrent of acceptance: you can't have faith but you have this. The Lord doesn't disappear when you turn away from Him; He remains, acknowledged in myriad forms, and even in the miracle of the ever shifting clouds themselves. The Lord is with you; no, He's not real. No, He's just a symbol. But this is such a potent symbol that your whole life is suddenly pervaded with Him. You belong to Him in the guise of art, and sensing something greater beyond it, though you haven't the courage or the ability yet to reach for what that is.

Lord, surely what I felt in that moment was love.

Faith, no. But love? Yes, love.

After visiting many gorgeous colonial churches in Rio, and viewing some of the most magnificent scenery in the world, we decided to wander around Brazil. For no particularly good reason we ended in Salvador da Bahia, a city that had been described to us by our friends in Rio.

And there we found two of the most intricate colonial churches that we were ever to see.

But to describe the impact of one of the the last churches I visited—to describe the way this pilgrimage to Brazil ended—I have to flash back to an afternoon in San Francisco many years before.

At the time, Stan and I were shopping in a store on Mission Street—the Mission Gift Shop—that sold religious statues, along with little white Communion dresses, and jewelry, largely for the Latin American families of the city. Mission

Street was their world. I was looking for religious collectibles. I wanted to have them around me. I wasn't sure why.

In this shop, I discovered an outrageous statue which at once riveted me; and I bought it, not even noticing what it cost.

The statue is about two feet high. It is a double statue, actually, because it includes Christ nailed to His cross, and beside Him the figure of St. Francis of Assisi, reaching up to embrace the Crucified Lord. But what makes the statue unique is that Our Lord is also reaching down from the cross to embrace Francis. Our Lord's right arm is freed from the cross and with this right arm, He tenderly holds the devoted saint.

This statue was made in Spain. It is hyperrealistic. Blood flows from Our Lord's wounds. His face is gaunt, stained with blood from His crown of thorns, and the blood from the crown flows down his shoulders onto His chest. He is looking down intently at the head of Francis who appears to be staring at the bloody wound in Our Lord's side.

Francis bears the wounds of the Stigmata in this statue. That is, Francis, too, has the wounds of the nails in his hands and in his feet. Francis was the first mystic ever to be granted the gift of the Stigmata. I knew this from childhood devotion to Francis. So this image made sense to me. What was new was the depiction of Our Lord reaching down to embrace Francis in this tender way.

The figures are graceful and delicate and they have dark skin.

The Lord's face is filled with love.

Francis, in this double statue, is in a brown robe—the

habit of his Franciscan Order—with a rope tied around his waist, and a wooden rosary hangs from this rope. Francis is barefoot. One wounded foot rests on a world globe without continents, a simple sphere of blue.

There are touching bits of ornamentation on these two figures—painted flowers on the loincloth of Our Lord, gold curlicues on the robe of Francis—an ornamentation that lifts them out of the bloody reality of the moment and renders them timeless and the property of all those who seek to possess the meaning of the union of Christ and the saint. An open book rests on the base of the statues, with words in Latin:

Qui-non Renuntiat Omnibus Que Possidet
Non Fotes Meus Esse Disipulus
LMC XVII

Never had I seen a statue that so reflected the disparate elements of my earlier faith. Here was the sensuality and excess and the spirituality which I had so loved.

I kept the statue on my desk as I wrote my "atheistic novels" and I defended it now and then against people who were understandably shocked by it, by its lurid embodiment of the suffering of the two figures.

Once I was even photographed holding the statue, and this photograph appeared in the *Village Voice*.

A deeper attachment to the statue involved my unresolved memory of the Catholic schoolgirl who had once prayed to Francis and to the Lord, who had once read excitedly the life of Francis, and who had once asked the Lord if He would not grant her the Stigmata—the visible signs of His wounds. I had prayed for that, yes. I had prayed for a mystical union with Our Lord, knowing full well that there is nothing one can do to "obtain" a mystical union with the Lord. A mystical union must be offered by God. And what greater visible sign of it could there be other than the wounds of the Stigmata?

Flash forward now to Salvador da Bahia, and a group of us walking up the steep hillside street to see two sensational colonial churches.

We turn in to one of these, and enter the inevitable captivating gloom, replete with the flicker of candles, the familiar envelope of lingering incense, and sumptuous detail.

And there on the distant altar, giant sized, is this very double statue, in exactly the same configuration. Francis embracing the crucified Lord. The Lord embracing Francis with His right arm.

I felt a great shock.

I felt I had journeyed all this way to Brazil and into the interior of Brazil to find this potent double image of the love of God. It was as if someone were whispering to me: This is not some statue you bought in a shop, and put among your collectibles. This is a figure of the love of Jesus Christ that is waiting for you. This is the mystery of the Incarnation. This is the Lord bridging the gulf between God and humankind. This is the Lord, in the midst of His atoning suffering, reaching out for . . . you.

I went back to the hotel, became sick with a blinding migraine, and did not go out again in Brazil.

In the next few years, if not before, I became convinced

that I was being pursued by the Lord. I did not think literally "He is pursuing me." After all, He wasn't supposed to exist. He was supposed to be an idea. He was "located" in nostalgia. I thought *something* is pursuing me. Something is *happening.*

I went to Italy again in 1998, and as before I visited church after church, returning again to Assisi, and visiting an ancient monastery where there was a thirteenth-century crucifix that drew me by its simplicity and its purity. While I was there, the feeling of being pursued continued.

One morning we went to a church in Rome specifically to see Bernini's great statue of St. Teresa of Avila because my son, Christopher, had studied this in school and wanted to see it firsthand. I put out of my mind, uncomfortably, my old love for St. Teresa, and my own special feelings about her ecstasy as represented so famously in this statue. Did anyone need to know I had once dreamed of entering the Carmelite nuns because of this great saint, that I had once lugged her autobiography around with me, struggling to read a few pages?

What would I do in this church? Well, I would look at the statue, and ask if there were any religious articles for sale, and I would buy as many of them as I could possibly carry.

Suddenly, while we were there, the priest came out with the altar boy and started to say Mass. Why Mass was being said at that time—very late in the morning—I had no idea. But there it was, the Mass being said in a partially empty church, in spite of a few milling tourists.

On our last day in Rome, we happened into St. Peter's

Basilica late in the evening. We wandered over the vast intricate marble floors. Then we realized Mass was being said, deep in the sanctuary.

Two of our party, who were Catholic, went up to hear Mass and I went with them. The music of the choir was transporting.

I had an overwhelming desire to go to Communion. But I could not do this. My two friends went to Communion and I sat there in the pew crying because I felt I could not do it. I was crushed and alone, and crying, in the heart of Christendom. I knew the rules too well to simply get up and approach the altar rail. And I did not want to offend my friends, who knew I was not a practicing Catholic, but even if they had not been there, I would not have gone. The pain of this moment was unforgettable. I felt I was not acknowledging something that I knew to be true; God was there. God was everywhere. God was God.

At home that year, it seemed that no matter when or how I turned on the television, images of the Mass flashed onto the screen. Mother Angelica had by that time created the great Catholic network, EWTN, and I was dimly aware of this, in spite of my aversion to all things Catholic; and in spite of that aversion, I found myself drawn to watching the Mass on EWTN.

Again and again I turned on the television to see the priest lifting the host at the moment of Consecration. I'd stop, sit down, and watch. This seemed to go well beyond coincidence, but it may well have been coincidence. Whatever the case, EWTN during those months became a constant reminder to me of my lost faith. Mother Angelica—whom, in my ignorance then, I regarded as an amusing little nun— was the Apostle who reached me during that year.

All this while, I continued to buy religious statues, to surround myself with the saints who'd once been the mentors of my childhood, and I continued to give support to the parish though I never set foot in the church.

The Vampire Armand and *Vittorio, The Vampire* are the two novels I wrote during the last year of my official atheism. Both reflect the conflict I was experiencing—the longing for reconciliation with God, and the inevitable despair that underscored the seeming impossibility of it.

But I should add, before I leave this chapter on the pilgrimages, on the pursuit, on the conflict—that no novel I wrote better reflects my longing for God than *Memnoch the Devil,* written several years before, in which my hero, the vampire Lestat, actually meets "God Incarnate" and his rebellious angel Memnoch, and is offered an opportunity to become part of the economy of salvation. Lestat rejects the offer, and flees from the purgatorial realm where souls prepare for acceptance into Heaven. But he carries out of this realm and back into the real world a particular article which has come into his hands earlier in the novel, on the road to Golgotha, where Lestat encountered Christ carrying His cross. The article is the legendary veil of Veronica, the veil that supposedly bears the image of Christ's blood-stained face.

The novel ends on a note of ambiguity: Were Lestat's visions of God and the Devil real? Or was Lestat the plaything of capricious spirits for whom Christianity is but one form of game? What is unambiguous at the close of the novel is the existence of Veronica's veil.

At the time I wrote the book, I saw the veil as causing confusion in the "real world" to which Lestat returned, evoking devotion and piety from a range of characters, whose actions could be viewed as irrational and hysterical at the worst.

I now feel differently about the veil in that novel. It is not the character of Lestat who rescued it from Time and brought it into the modern world. It is the author who grabbed hold of it, and fled from moral confusion in the novel with the Face of Christ on the veil in her hands. It is the author who held it up for all to see, and then backed away, deep into the fictional matrix, leaving its meaning unresolved.

Now it's time to speak of my conversion, my return to faith, my return to the loving—and eternally outstretched—arms of the Lord.

8

As I've explained earlier, my faith in atheism was cracking. I went through the motions of being a conscientious atheist, trying to live without religion, but in my heart of hearts, I was losing faith in the "nothingness," losing faith in "the absurd."

Understand, we were living contentedly in New Orleans, among secular and Catholic friends and family. There was no pressure from anyone to *do anything* about this issue, this matter of faith. There was no zealot at the door or at the coffee table pounding away about how I should come home to my church. Far from it. To repeat, I was surrounded by tolerant Catholics, and Catholics who were no longer shunning those who didn't conform.

And I'd noticed other things about these Catholics. Minor things, I should say, but they are worth noting. These

Catholics did not always stay married for life; they got annulments; and they remarried with the approval of their church. And these Catholics were not having thirteen children like my great-grandmother Josephine Becker Curry, nor were they having nine children like my grandmother Bertha Curry O'Brien, nor were they even having six or seven children. They were Catholics through and through but they had smaller families, and that indicated to me that there had been changes within the Catholic Church of which I wasn't aware.

These observations weren't a determining factor in the return of my faith. But they did suggest that the church of my childhood was somehow more inclusive and accepting than it had been. Not only was the Latin gone, perhaps a certain rigid attitude towards sex was gone as well.

I didn't inquire too closely about all this. I'd asked a few questions here and there, as I've mentioned, but in general this aspect of things didn't much matter.

There was a storm in my heart and soul that had little to do with other people and their decisions. I held out against God and I held out against the church because I thought I was holding out for bitter truth.

But history was telling me every day there could very well be a God. The story of the survival of the Jews told me that there could very well be a God. Everything I was reading—and I was reading more than ever before—was telling me in a secret and insistent voice: Anne, you know there is a God.

Even my time among the skeptics, present and past, sang to me—in memory—of God. In California, as I'd listened to the passionate stories of civil rights workers or war protestors,

I'd heard the voice of conscience, the commitment to high principles, the deep-rooted need to do "good." No one I ever met was indifferent to conscience or to acute moral responsibility. I saw no evidence even in the most strident anti-religious talk of people who didn't believe in something, who didn't suffer inwardly for those beliefs.

One afternoon I accosted my son, Christopher, on the staircase and demanded, "Do you believe in God?"

Here was a young man not yet twenty, brought up to believe in nothing, and in that time of life when beliefs are most easily dismissed. And Christopher, after a moment's reflection, responded, "Yes, I believe in God."

How could that have happened? How could our free-thinking son believe in God?

The creation was talking to me of God. My visceral responses to the purple evening sky, to the canopy of oak branches that sheltered our front steps, to the flowers blooming beyond garden fences—my most cherished memories of the beauty of Port-au-Prince, Haiti, or Rio de Janeiro, or Venice, Italy—all this was speaking to me of God.

The music of a violin sang to me of God. The great paintings of Giotto and Rembrandt spoke to me of God. An intense study of the lives of various composers spoke to me of God. Giotto's angels, those desperate, sobbing angels crying to Heaven as they witnessed the Crucifixion in Giotto's painting—they cried and cried for the love of God.

The world around me was filled to the brim with God.

And the person of Jesus Christ—the mystery of Jesus and how He'd started a worldwide religion—this weighed on my

"rational" mind. *Who was He really? Who had He been?*
Why was twentieth-century America so obsessed with Him?
Twentieth-century America certainly wasn't living in a post-
Christian world! Why did people flock by the thousands
to the musical *Jesus Christ Superstar?* Why in the world did
Americans become so furious over the film *The Last Tempta-
tion of Christ?* Why were there plastic Jesuses on dashboards,
and why was His name the most common "curse word"
I heard? Why was it the most common curse word that I
myself spoke?

America appeared obsessed with Jesus Christ. Why?
I mean, almost two thousand years had passed since Christ
had come into the world; and a host of modern thinkers
had declared that religion had no validity, or to put it more
poetically: God was dead. My skeptical friends had long ago
declared that religion hadn't a particle of energy left to it. I'd
agreed with them. I'd said so in my novels. Didn't my venerable immortal Marius hold forth at length on the demise of
"revealed religion" and the marvelous opportunities for the
rational world that were to follow this long overdue and
ignominious death? I'd said so to anyone who asked me.
I'd said so to myself. Why, religion was dying out in 1998,
wasn't it?

So why this nationwide obsession with the Son of God?

What was the driving force here behind the Jesus who
wouldn't go away? The story of the Incarnation—the story of
an absolute and all-powerful God who became Man to be
with us—began to obsess me as something unique in the history of the ancient religions I constantly studied.

Of course, I'd read plenty about the ancient mystery cults, the celebrations of the dying vegetation god, and his resurrection each year in the new crops; I'd studied the goddess Isis with the child Horus in her arms—an iconic forerunner of the Virgin and the Baby Jesus which had dominated art for over fifteen hundred years. And I knew the old Catholic arguments—that these religious rituals and ideas and symbols *prefigured* the Lord Jesus Christ and His entry into history. I saw the logic of that. I also saw that, similar though they were, these ancient religious rituals were only vaguely like the story of the Incarnation. They did not involve the God of All Creation becoming one of us.

I came to be in awe of the unique power of the story of the Incarnation. To hell with all I'd studied. I began to sense that I was being blinded day in and day out by an inexplicable light. I lived my life as if it weren't shining down on me, but it was shining down. It was breaking forth out of the shadows of every matrix of ideas or images that I examined. It was searing my shivering heart.

My own writings took me again and again and again to God. In *The Vampire Armand,* the talk of the Incarnation of Christ is relentless. *Blood and Gold* was obsessed with the tension between kinds of religious fervor. The broken heart of *Pandora* has to do with that character's loss of all sense of the religious—her capitulation, under pressure, to living in a godless world.

Talk of God was the private feverish sound of my own mind.

I drifted through the contemporary world, blind as usual

to whatever was happening politically or religiously, thinking about these seemingly timeless ideas. If readers didn't see or value the focus on this in my novels, well, that was no surprise. So much else was going on in the books; my methods were those of submersion and surrender. I'd always been willing to subject myself to a book to the degree that the writing of it could drive me almost out of my mind.

I was Christ haunted.

I was thinking again and again of the famous lines of the poet Francis Thompson:

I fled Him, down the nights and down the days;
I fled Him, down the arches of the years;
I fled Him, down the labyrinthine ways
    Of my own mind; and in the mist of tears
I hid from Him, and under running laughter.
      Up vistaed hopes I sped;
      And shot, precipitated,
Adown Titanic glooms of chasmèd fears,
    From those strong Feet that followed, followed after.
      But with unhurrying chase,
      And unperturbèd pace,
Deliberate speed, majestic instancy,
      They beat—and a Voice beat
      More instant than the Feet—
"All things betray thee, who betrayest Me."

Long years ago, in high school, I'd memorized this poem. It had been my father's favorite poem, my father who had spent his youth in the Redemptorist Seminary at Kirkwood, Missouri. Now it was part of a deafening chorus of voices singing the songs of God to me as I struggled with myriad doubts, myriad fears, and, seemingly, alone.

Yet I clung to my atheism; I clung with a martyr's determination. Why? Because I still believed it was "the truth." And I lacked any systematic approach to the problems that were tearing me apart.

Finally in December of 1998, on the afternoon of Sunday, the sixth, everything—for me—changed. It was the first of two small miracles I was to experience before the anniversary of Our Lord's birth.

My diary doesn't give me much help as to what happened on that day. My notes are factual and simple:

> *This is a happy day for me—my reconciliation to the Church. . . . I read a lot of St. Augustine last night. What poetry. I'm also reading on purgatory. Jacques Le Goff. . . I feel peace and quiet in my soul. I feel happiness. I think—I know—Stan is happy for me. He told me.*

The note for December 7 reads:

> *Went to Mass and Holy Communion. Received Our Lord into my body and heart for the first time in thirty-eight years. . . . I went to the side altar of the Giant Crucifix and said my special prayers of thanks to God for giving me the Gift of Faith and the strength to do this. . . . I was so nervous. When the priest put the host in my hand, I didn't*

know whether he had finished speaking or not. Then to put it in my mouth was easy. Only in the pew did I find a private moment to feel Christ inside me and to cry a little, spontaneously. I didn't want to make a scene.

Several paragraphs later:

My mind was on Mass and Communion. I love the story of the Incarnation so much—the idea of a God who becomes a man for love.

The entry for Saturday, December 12, 1998, includes this:

I am married in the church. We married at the altar of St. Mary's Assumption Church on Constance and Josephine.

Scribbled in the back of the diary, only a few pages later, are these words that I must have written some time before:

> *My heart is good but I am a monster. . . .*
> *I'm not without a soul.*
>
> —Le Bête. Beauty and the Beast.
> *Cocteau*

The diary ends there.

The second small miracle—which occurred on December 14, 1998, is not described in the diary at all.

That day was a Monday on which I slipped into a diabetic

coma and was rushed to the hospital, with a blood sugar level of over eight hundred, and a heart that was ceasing to beat. I was unconscious as a team of doctors tried to save my life. And save my life they somehow did. That miracle is simple to explain. Without knowing it, I had become a type 1 diabetic. At some point—probably around September of that year—my pancreas had all but shut down its production of insulin. For months I'd been sick with diabetes. Without knowing it, I'd almost died.

The first of the small miracles—how I managed to approach the Lord through the doors of the Roman Catholic Church—is a great deal more complex and will take a good many more words to describe.

9

WHAT HAPPENS WHEN FAITH RETURNS? What happens when one goes back to the church of one's childhood?

I've described part of the first miracle of December 6, 1998, before—in print, and many a time in interviews, and sometimes to those who have casually asked: How did you come to believe in God again? What caused you to do this?

It's important to try now to describe this "conversion" or "return" once again, perhaps in a fresh way.

When I go back to the very moment—that Sunday afternoon—what I recall most vividly is surrender—a determination to give in to something deeply believed and deeply felt. I loved God. I loved Him with my whole heart. I loved Him in the Person of Jesus Christ, and I wanted to go back to Him.

I remember vaguely that I was sitting at my desk in a dreadfully cluttered office, hemmed in on all sides by rows and stacks of books, and that I had little sense of anything but the desire to surrender to that overwhelming love.

I knew that the German church of my childhood, St. Mary's Assumption, was perhaps six blocks away from where I was sitting. And perhaps I remembered my mother's words of decades ago. "He is on that altar. Get up and go." I know now when I think of those moments in 1998, I hear her voice. I see her dimly, rousing us, telling us to get up and get dressed and "go to Mass."

What confounded me and silenced me in 1998 was that I believed that what she'd said so many years ago was precisely the truth. He *was* in that church. He *was* on that altar. And I wanted to go to Him, and the impelling emotion was love.

Only dimly did I care about the doctrine of the Transubstantiation, the Catholic teaching as to how Our Blessed Lord is present Body and Blood in the small wafers kept in the Catholic tabernacle. Only dimly did I reflect on it, because truly I had a sense of something so much greater than the verbal expression of any one doctrine that it didn't matter to me how superstitious such a belief might seem to a skeptical mind. And my mind was still, to some extent, a skeptical mind.

I didn't care about the framing of the doctrine. I cared about Him. And He was calling me back through His Presence on the altar. He might have used the falling rain to call me back; He might have used the music of Vivaldi. He might have used the statue of Christ and Francis that was on my desk. But, no, He used the doctrine of the Real Presence.

And I surrendered to that doctrine because it was the way

to Him, and He was what I wanted, with my heart and soul. Go to Him, I thought. Go to the Christ who is under the roof of your church. He's waiting there for you. Get up from the desk and go. Go to the Christ who is Real and Present in every Catholic tabernacle throughout the world. Go to Him.

In the moment of surrender, I let go of all the theological or social questions which had kept me from Him for countless years. I simply let them go. There was the sense, profound and wordless, that if He knew everything I did not have to know everything, and that, in seeking to know everything, I'd been, all of my life, missing the entire point.

No social paradox, no historic disaster, no hideous record of injustice or misery should keep me from Him. No question of Scriptural integrity, no torment over the fate of this or that atheist or gay friend, no worry for those condemned and ostracized by my church or any other church should stand between me and Him. The reason? It was magnificently simple: He knew how or why *everything* happened; He knew the disposition of *every single soul.*

He wasn't going to let anything happen by accident! Nobody was going to go to Hell by mistake. This was His world, all this! He had complete control of it; His justice, His mercy—were not our justice or our mercy. What folly to even imagine such a thing.

I didn't have to know how He was going to save the unlettered and the unbaptized, or how He would redeem the conscientious heathen who had never spoken His name. I didn't have to know how my gay friends would find their way to Redemption; or how my hardworking secular humanist

friends could or would receive the power of His Saving
Grace. I didn't have to know why good people suffered agony
or died in pain. He knew.

And it was His *knowing* that overwhelmed me, His *knowing* that became completely real to me, His *knowing* that
became the warp and woof of the Universe which He had
made.

His was—after all—the Divine Mind which had made
the miracle of the Big Bang, and created the DNA only lately
discovered in every physical cell. His was the Divine Mind
that had created the sound of the violin in the Beethoven
concerto; His was the Divine Mind that made snowflakes,
candle flames, birds soaring upwards, the unfolding mystery
of gender, and the gravity that seemingly held the Universe
together—as our planet, our single little planet, hurtled
through space.

Of course. If He could do all that, *naturally* He knew the
answer to every conceivable question before it was formulated. He knew the worst suffering that a human soul could
feel. Nothing was wasted with Him because He was the
author of all of it. He was the Creator of creatures who felt
anger, alienation, rage, despair. In this great novel that was
His creation, He knew every plot, every character, every
action, every voice, every syllable, and every jot of ink.

And why should I remain apart from Him just because I
couldn't grasp all this? He could grasp it. Of course!

It was love that brought me to this awareness, love that
brought me into a complete trust in Him, a trust that God
who made us could not ever abandon us—that the seeming

meaninglessness of our world was the limit of our understanding, but never, never the limit of His.

Words fail. They have to fail. How can I describe this trust and this abandon, this realization that He was capable of righting every wrong? Ah, I have to say more than that. How can I describe the realization that He was the Divine Safety Net through which nothing could accidentally fall?

This is a mystical thing that I'm trying to analyze; it is a transcendent moment when one senses with all one's faculties that the love of God is the air we breathe.

It was only as I felt this love and this trust, that I realized I believed in Him. It was only in love and trust that belief followed—and all became part of the complete surrender: go to Him, go with Him. Pass out of resistance into Him. This will not be easy; this will not bring comfort. This is not going to make you feel good. This is going to be hard! But this is where you must go.

I mean how in the world was I to live with Roman Catholicism again and all of its many rules? I wasn't even sure anymore what those rules were. How was I going to go back to a religion that my sophisticated friends despised and denigrated, that some of the finer minds I'd known regarded with blatant contempt? How was I to become a card-carrying member of a church that condemned my gay son?

No, it was not the path of least resistance; it was not a falling into simple happiness. And no irresistible surge of emotional triumph carried me through this decision. If anything it took a draining stamina, to get up from the desk and to move towards Him. It certainly took an act of faith that

He would somehow make this return possible for me, He would show me how to live once more with creeds and codes that had once driven me half out of my mind.

It didn't really matter how wretched it was going to be. I had to go! I wasn't going to deny Him any longer. I was going *home.*

And here is where the first "miracle" of that year comes into play. Bear with me. This I have never described before and it deserves describing.

I wanted Him! I wanted to be with Him, and talk to Him, and kneel before Him, and open my soul to Him, and the place that I sought Him was indeed that ancient Roman Catholic Church.

But, as I have said, I didn't know anything about the recent history of that church. And, as a result, I was sublimely ignorant of a multitude of things the knowledge of which just might have crippled me and confused me at this crucial moment and left me stunned and unable to proceed.

It was a beautiful ignorance. It was the true miracle of which I speak.

Had I known, for example, of the church's firm stand against the ordination of women, of the documents in which its teachings have been worked out and the degree to which these statements have been declared unchangeable, I might have been far too disheartened to proceed.

Had I known of the extent of the annulment process and how elaborate it had become, and how common, and how often Catholic marriages of ten to twenty years were being declared null and void, and never to have existed, I would probably have been too perplexed to know which way to turn.

Had I known the extent of the ever broadening pedophilia scandal in my church, I might have been too saddened and discouraged to take a step.

Had I read any of the *Theology of the Body*, with its strong emphasis on gender roles and gender complementarity, I might have been utterly brokenhearted and unable to move on.

Had I known of the bitter polarization between the right and left in my church after Vatican II, I might have been repelled and wounded, and unable to draw close to the church doors.

But the miracle was: I didn't know any of these things! Not a single one of them.

And I didn't even know the name of the present pope.

All I knew—thankfully and with tears—was that the great and ancient Roman Catholic Church of my childhood was still there! And that seemed the miracle for the moment, not what I didn't know.

And so I went back to God through the doors of that church, returning to Him through the sacrament of Confession, with the kind understanding of a brilliant and thoroughly Catholic priest who spoke the mother tongue of my religion with beauty that I could hear and receive and comprehend.

I went back to the ancient Roman Catholic Church of Christ Our Lord who was crucified, died and buried, and rose on the Third Day. I went back to the Catholic Church of

St. Paul and the Apostles, and the angels Gabriel, Michael, Raphael. I went back to the church of the Blessed Virgin Mary, first among the saved. I went back to the church of St. Augustine and his mother, St. Monica; of St. Jerome and St. Patrick. I went back to the church of St. Francis of Assisi and the painter Giotto; back to the church of St. Teresa of Avila and the music of Palestrina; back to the church of St. Joan of Arc and the music of Andrea Gabrieli; back to the church of Michelangelo and Antonio Vivaldi, the church of Ignatius Loyola and St. Alphonsus, the church of sweet St. Thérèse, The Little Flower, with the bouquet of roses in her arms. And above all, I went back to the ancient Roman Catholic Church of the Apostolic Succession which held as solemn truth that Christ was Real and Present in the Blessed Sacrament on the altar. This was "the rock pitched into space" that Monsignor Fulton J. Sheen had once described. This was the Eternal Church of the Lord.

And so it was a return to the Romanesque dome and the Gothic arch, to the stained-glass windows, to plainsong and Verdi's Requiem, to the priest with the white wafer in his hands, and to the beaming Christ Child in his crib of straw.

Yes, this was the way home through the doors of the Eternal Church, with its marble floors, and painted saints, its solemn icon of Our Mother of Perpetual Help, and its unmistakable incense, its ever faithful candles, its soft and fragrant flowers, its draped altars, its golden tabernacle doors.

Lord, I'm here.

That was the first and foremost miracle of 1998 for me— the miracle of knowing and unknowing, the miracle of trust, the miracle of love, the miracle of what didn't matter, the miracle of faith, and the miracle of surrender and the miracle of return.

> *Halts by me that footfall—*
> *Is my gloom, after all,*
> *Shade of His hand, outstretched caressingly?*
> *"Ah, fondest, blindest, weakest,*
> *I am He Whom thou seekest!*
> *Thou dravest love from thee, who dravest Me."*

—Francis Thompson,
"The Hound of Heaven"

10

It wasn't until the summer of 2002 that my commitment to Jesus Christ became complete.

From December 1998 on, however, my commitment to believing in Him, to worshipping Him, and to keeping to the doctrines of the Roman Catholic Church was strong.

I have already stated that my return to Christ, my return to Him through the doors of the Roman Catholic Church, was not something simple. It was not a collapsing into consolation or happiness.

And I want to stress this again.

It seems to me that many people think a Christian conversion is exactly that—a falling into simplicity; a falling from intellect into an emotional refuge; an attempt to feel good. There are even writers today who see Christian conversion as a form of empowerment, and books are written that promise born-again Christians not only complete peace of mind, but even monetary gain.

My return involved complete trust in God, an admission of faith in Him, a faith made evident by love. But it took an iron will to go back to Him. I anticipated grave difficulties. I feared grave obligations. And I was in no way able to turn against the secular humanist friends and teachers and culture which I had for so many years admired.

I, who all my adult life had been a member of nothing, had to become a member of this something, and it took all the will that I had.

When I recovered from the diabetic coma that almost killed me, when I gradually worked my way back to health, I experienced a dry period in which faith for the moment did not make sense. I did not cease to believe in God. Rather, recovering as I was from the severe mental effects of ketoacidosis—in which the brain actually shrinks and gradually has to restore itself—I felt frightened by my new commitment, and it was only with great difficulty that I went back to Mass.

The first task that confronted me was to learn the Mass in English, to learn to participate in it aloud as Catholics of our time now do.

The idea of the English Mass was distasteful. I grieved inordinately for the old Latin—the beautiful Tridentine Mass on which I'd been brought up—and it seemed an immense tragedy to me that the service was so changed, and that the magnificent hymns of my childhood were apparently almost entirely gone.

But I was determined to learn the new Mass. I was there for the Lord, and I was there as a Catholic. And I was bound and determined to do what was required.

I soon settled into a weekly regimen of attending the Saturday Vigil Mass rather than the Sunday morning Mass—something easier for me during my physical recovery—and I took my place in the front pew of the church, not because I wanted to be seen, or to feel important, but because I wanted no distractions as I followed the movements and gestures of the priest and the altar server in front of me.

St. Mary's Church, as I believe I mentioned earlier, had been built by the German immigrants of our parish. And during my childhood it had operated right alongside St. Alphonsus, the church built by the Irish. But now St. Alphonsus was no longer a consecrated church at all but a prized historical monument being used for other purposes, and so St. Mary's was the parish church to which I had to go.

Whereas St. Alphonsus is in the Romanesque style, St. Mary's is Gothic, but certainly no less magnificent than St. Alphonsus, and in fact it houses an altar of uncommon intricacy and beauty because it is made up of so many statues of so many Apostles, angels, and saints. The altar even includes a huge and ornate depiction in plaster of God the Father, seated on His Heavenly Throne, with Christ sitting beside Him, and beneath them the Virgin Mary being crowned as Queen of Heaven.

Before Mass and even in moments after it, the contemplation of the details of this altar gave me a supreme pleasure. I was home, yes, home, amid images I understood, and let me say once again—because it's so important—I never confused these images with the entities that they represented. Rather I gazed on them to be reminded of things eternal, and things which I now felt "free" to study and experience to the full.

But the most vital part of my reeducation was hearing the Mass spoken aloud by the priest and by those of us in the pews, indeed hearing words of it spoken aloud by me—and focusing for the first time on words which decades ago had been buried in the printed missal.

In other words, prayer was once again acoustic for me rather than something read. Reeducation in Christ was acoustic and gave my mind an immediate and powerful sequence of impressions of the sort I'd never really been able to gain so easily from books.

Also this weekly Mass involved singing. And though the congregation was small, and mostly made up of elderly people, there was a gifted cantor, a soprano named Sheila, who sang with operatic power and grace.

My first full participation came through singing the "Gloria" with Sheila—the hymn I described earlier in this book. Whatever grief I felt for the old Latin was soon burnt away by the power of this hymn, guided as it was by the soprano's clear and soaring voice.

The most moving verse of the "Gloria" for me, as we sung it, was:

For You alone are the Holy One,
You alone are the Lord,
You alone are the Most High,

Jesus Christ,
With the Holy Spirit,
In the glory of God the Father.
Amen.

It was possible to look up, as I sang these words, and look at the statues of God the Father, and the Lord Jesus Christ, and the Holy Spirit, in the form of a dove, hovering above them.

I wish I could convey what it meant to sing this hymn because I wasn't just singing it with my voice; I was singing it with my will. I was abandoning my will, no matter how bitter my fears, to the sentiments expressed in this hymn. Week after week as I sang the words "You alone are the Lord," I would feel chills over my entire body. It seemed I had come home to something of incalculable power. And there was the opportunity, *the opportunity,* after decades of silence to pour out in song the love I felt.

My education involved another extraordinary prayer which we spoke aloud, a prayer I'd never noticed in my childhood: the Nicene Creed.

As we stood to recite this—after the sermon and before the Liturgy of the Eucharist—I found myself speaking the most fascinating and evocative words, words written in A.D. 325 as the result of the first church council convened by the Emperor Constantine, a council at which Christians reached a consensus on their Christological beliefs. But I didn't care about that history. I didn't care about all the arguments as to how consensus was achieved, and whether or not it was valid, or what it meant that hundreds of men would come together to hammer out a litany of beliefs in contradiction to other men.

What struck me was the profundity of the words we had, from those early times, received and preserved.

The very first verse ended in a line of shocking beauty:

> *We believe in one God,*
> *The Father, the Almighty,*
> *Maker of heaven and earth,*
> *Of all that is seen and unseen.*

"Of all that is seen and unseen." The simplicity of this hit me with great force. But the next and longer verse was equally mesmerizing and exalting:

> *We believe in one Lord, Jesus Christ,*
> *The only Son of God,*
> *Eternally begotten of the Father,*
> *God from God, Light from Light,*
> *True God from true God,*
> *Begotten, not made, one in Being with the Father.*
> *Through Him all things were made.*

These words alone gave me enough to think about for the rest of my life. Of course I knew they represented controversy and accommodation, men arguing with men. So what? They represented a grappling with the Absolute which perfectly reflected my own intellectual struggles for nearly forty years.

I loved these words. I loved that every week we were going to say them aloud, that we were going to stand there in communion, all of us in the church, and speak these words aloud together.

It's conceivable that the Apostles' Creed, known so well to me from childhood, had become dead to me, and that this Nicene Creed was giving me a fresh immersion in what I truly did believe.

The English Mass went on to yield other treasures.

The experience of the Consecration of the Eucharist was far more vital and wondrous than it had ever been for me in the old Latin days. The Memorial Acclamation that we sang together before the raised Body and Blood had a subtle triumphant power:

Christ has died, Christ is risen, Christ will come again.

Finally when the priest sang the doxology:

Through him, with him, in him, in the unity of the Holy Spirit, all glory and honor is yours, almighty Father, for ever and ever, we answered with the reverent song of the Great Amen.

Never before had I recited the Lord's Prayer with others in such a solemn way. We held hands at Mass as we said it; we spoke it in unison and with a full commitment to every word.

> *Our Father, Who art in Heaven,*
> *hallowed be Thy name;*
> *Thy kingdom come,*
> *Thy will be done,*
> *on earth as it is in Heaven.*

Give us this day our daily bread;
and forgive us our trespasses,
as we forgive those who trespass against us,
and lead us not into temptation,
but deliver us from evil.

In sum, this prayer, which I had rushed through a million times in childhood, now unfolded for me, on my own lips, as utterly splendid and richly meaningful.

Afterwards, to turn to others, to clasp their hands, to wish them "the peace of Christ," to embrace them—this was hard for an old guard Catholic who had never done such a thing during Mass; but it too was immensely powerful. And a palpable love spread throughout the church, an undeniable warmth and sense of true community.

Along with these new experiences there came the old ones as well, including the singing of what we'd called the Agnus Dei:

Lamb of God, You take away the sins of the world: have mercy on us.

Communion itself was a bit of a shock. Instead of receiving the host on our tongues from the consecrated fingers of the priest, we received the wafer in our hands, and placed it in our mouths on our own. But even this had an intimate beauty to it, a new dignity. It was also possible to drink the consecrated wine from the chalice, something quite new for me, but this I chose not to do.

When I returned to the pew, after receiving Communion, my prayers were almost entirely shaped by awe—by the continuous song from my heart of gratitude that I'd been invited back to the banquet, that I was once again receiving Christ as He had told us to receive Him at the Last Supper. The words from the Gospels that best characterize the emotions I felt are those from the Gospel of John, which Jesus speaks to His Apostles:

Remain in Me, as I remain in you.

Time spent at Mass during these years of learning the new ways was blissful time, no matter how dry I felt, no matter how estranged from consolation. I had discovered vital and unshakable connections between the new English Mass and the old Latin Mass, and there was never any feeling in me that I was not in my church.

I felt united with God again; I felt empowered to talk to Him, to discuss with Him the difficulties of my day-to-day existence, and to put before Him in intimate conversation my confusion about the novels I wrote, and how little they reflected my new change in faith.

My life wasn't easy, by any means, during the years 1999, 2000, and 2001. The novels I wrote reflected the gradual fragmentation of my old alienated vision. I no longer felt complete writing supernatural fiction about metaphorical beings shut out of salvation. I wanted to talk more about my relationship with God.

As for my life day in and day out, I'm not sure it reflected by any means my complete devotion to God. I lived, pretty much as I'd lived before, an unusual public and private life in New Orleans, writing and reading for long hours in my study, breaking for publicity tours to support my new novels, and presiding over huge family reunions at Mardi Gras and at Christmas, seeking to play some meaningful role in the lives of my family members, and yet confused as to what my new novels meant.

No special demand was made on me by my newfound faith. When anyone tried to argue with me about it, I simply refused to discuss it. So I was no evangelist among the unconverted. And I was still prey to long periods of depression and morbidity which seemed as much a part of my personality as type 1 diabetes was a part of my physical life.

The novel *Blackwood Farm* was my principal accomplishment during this period, and it proved to be a strange novel indeed. It involved my vampire heroes and heroines, and even some of the characters from my earlier novels about the Mayfair Witches, but there was a strange blending of the old elements with new religious sentiments. Indeed I think the book can be seen as two novels trying to break apart from each other: one about the real world of the South as I knew it, with its big families and its unique characters; and the other a supernatural novel about the old themes of being ripped out of the world of grace into the world of darkness against one's will.

Blackwood Farm, the place itself—a fabulous bed-and-breakfast mansion in rural Mississippi—clearly represented a redemptive world that was almost a state of mind. The vampire characters impinged on it, seeking to destroy it. But Blackwood Farm persevered as a household where people could and did love in a Christian spirit. Idealized human characters dominated the book at the expense of the supernatural predators. The forces of good, personified by the family of Quinn Blackwood, gain a power they lacked in any of my previous work.

In sum, I was pulling away from my old writing because I didn't identify anymore with the theologically marginalized and the alienated; and I didn't know quite what to do about this change in myself. And so the book reflects the dilemma, the wrestling, the confusion, and the strong insistence that we do live in a world where redemption is possible and where Christian values can supplant the compromises of despair.

In spite of all this, the glamorous forces of evil do overtake Quinn Blackwood. I did not succeed in creating a world for him in which the vampires and witches of my past work would be banished for his sake. So it is a book about an aesthetic war and a spiritual war which I lost.

11

As the year 2002 began, I wasn't aware of living a particularly Christian life for God. I didn't live an unchristian life. But I had not truly been transformed in Christ. I was a churchgoer for God. I was a committed Catholic. Nothing kept me from weekly Mass and Communion, but my participation in the age-old ritual of the Mass was still the fullest expression of my Catholic life.

I should say here that I was keenly aware that my age had made my conversion easy for me. I was past the age of childbearing. I was married to my childhood sweetheart, who had graciously consented to marrying me in my church. Therefore I faced no agonizing questions as to how to be a Catholic day in and day out. I didn't confront the church's teachings on birth control or abortion. I didn't confront the church's teachings on any particular form of excess because mine was a fairly conventional life. I didn't smoke, drink, or gamble. I spent some time—and I hesitate to mention this for obvious reasons but I think it is germane here—I spent some time trying to give away some of the money I made to others for whom it might make a difference, and I contributed to the support of my church. But these things I'd done before my conversion.

Secular humanist values had always prompted me to try to share some of the benefits I received as the result of my writing. I was a committed Democrat, and it was part of my Democratic Party consciousness that I provide medical insurance for my employees and that I pay the premium for them and for their dependents. I can't claim any of this was specifically Christian.

I wasn't really "born again" in Christ, so much as I was home again and safe in Christ, and the only subject really weighing on my mind was that of my writing, that it reflect more my current beliefs.

The pedophilia scandal began to make national news. Catholic priests were accused of molesting teenagers and sometimes children.

This was an ugly and demoralizing matter for Catholics. I didn't want to believe this had happened. I didn't want to believe the scope of the problem. In sum, I didn't want to face that such a pattern of behavior could have existed among our clergy. And it prompted me, for the first time, to do some reading about the present church.

I chose not to read about the scandal itself, though there were no doubt responsible books in circulation about the priests accused of molesting children. I wasn't ready to confront the material. I chose rather to read something of the recent history of Catholicism—a subject I'd always avoided in the past.

My approach was historical to the point of being musty. I wanted to know what sort of men ran the church today, as opposed, say, to the type of men who'd run it in the Middle Ages, or the eleventh century.

So I read a big thick biography of the present pope. I read the biographies of the popes before him. And I took away from this reading the simple conclusion that these were pious and dedicated men. Pope John Paul II, Pope Paul VI, and Pope John XXIII were men of unquestioned holiness. All right. Things were good at the top. That is what I wanted to know. The church would weather this pedophilia scandal as it had weathered other scandals. The church would reform itself. It had to reform itself. Even as a little Catholic girl, I'd known the church was constantly reforming itself. It was "the rock pitched into space" and nothing would halt its progress.

Of course, these books took me through some of the recent moral controversies that had affected the church—the birth control crisis under Pope Paul VI; the ordination of women rejected by John Paul II—but I didn't pay much attention to these issues, and I did not have the theological preparation necessary to tackle the entire question of Vatican II and its many documents and what these documents had meant for the church.

But reading about the piety of the popes had a particular personal effect on me. It tended to remind me of my own early inclinations as a Catholic, to give my life totally to God. As I read about the vocation and dedication of Paul VI, I revisited my own childhood desire to be a priest, and then to be a nun.

My reading began to include more devotional books; and I became fascinated with the Stigmata: the means by which a saint or holy person receives the wounds of Christ.

Of course I still had my lovely and much cherished statue of St. Francis of Assisi reaching up to embrace the Crucified Lord. And I knew well the story of how Francis had received, in a vision, the wounds in his own hands and feet.

I remembered palpably a time in my youth when I had said to God, "Thy will be done." I knew now how limited had been my sense of humility; sanctity had been connected in my mind with adventure and great achievement, and even fame.

Yet the softer, more richly colored aspects of that childhood fervor came back to me. There had been a time when truly I had wanted to give everything to the Lord. There had been a time when I thought nothing less than this was acceptable.

How could I do this now? How could I say to the Lord, "Thy will be done" when I had forty-nine employees and a family? What was this negotiation that was going on between me and my Blessed Lord?

Sometime in the summer of 2002, I began to talk to God about this whole question. I began to talk with Him about how far I was willing to go in devoting my life to Him. And the question of the Stigmata obsessed me. Was I willing to say to God, "Do with me what you will"? What if He were to visit the wounds of the Stigmata on me?

Understand, I didn't think any such miracle was in the offing. Who was I to be visited with the Stigmata? But the point was: could I say to the Lord, Do what you will and I will accept it? Who was I as a follower of Christ? And just what was a follower of Christ, after all?

As a child, I'd once pledged my life in its entirety. What would I do now if the Lord asked of me that I come and follow Him? How was I going to walk away from the support of my family, forty-nine employees, two condominiums, and five buildings?

My conversations with God during those quiet moments in the pew before Mass were becoming ruminations.

"Lord," I was saying, "I'm writing another book, and well, this book is really going to be for you and about you, but it will contain the old motifs and some of the old characters, and of course strike some people as profane, that's bound to happen, but Lord, this is my bread and butter, and Lord, it's the bread and butter of quite a number of other people, too. No, I can't say, 'Do what you will with me.' How can I say this? I have too many people to take care of, including myself."

This had become, as I recall, a regular rambling. "Lord, what does it mean to belong to you? Lord, you came here for us, you lived amongst us, you died for us! And rose amongst us. What does it mean that I love you, that I am yours?"

How abstract and symbolic were the thoughts of the Stigmata! If God chose me for such an honor, I'd have to refuse. I have to write with these hands, don't I? Where was the Catholic girl who would not have said no to anything? She wasn't a mere victim of childhood enthusiasms and illusions. She was someone who still resided in me.

And she had known that barriers to the priesthood meant nothing when the Lord chose to gift the Stigmata to His servants. To those whom the Lord gifted with His revelations and His visions, opportunities were given which far surpassed any Holy Orders offered by His church.

I believed in God. I feared Him. I feared what He might ask of me. I saw the shallowness of my commitment. I saw the incompleteness of my love. Mine was a negotiated abandonment, and that meant it was not a true abandonment at all.

I don't recall talking to anyone about this. It was too intensely personal to share with another. And how pompous and foolish it might have sounded over a café table. *What if God wants something more of me? I'm afraid.*

"Why would God want something more from you?" a critic might have demanded. "Who the hell are you? Why should God care?"

I cared. Untutored, confused, I was privy to a remembered devotion and a wisdom that informed it, and had never let me forget it over all these years.

Then one Saturday afternoon, everything changed. The change was as dramatic as the change of December 6, 1998, but I didn't know it. I was seated in the pew and going through The Great Negotiation—what I gave and what I didn't give, what I wanted to do, and what I feared to do. And then the simplest of solutions occurred to me: *Write for God. Write for Him. Write only for Him.*

Begin now, as you walk out of this church after Mass, to be a writer only for Him. Take whatever talent you have, and experience you've acquired, and put them to work strictly and entirely for Him. Never write another word that is not for Him. Write His life! Write for Him.

Broken being that I am, I did not implement this commitment until December of that year. But the Consecration was made that summer afternoon, and a veil was lifted from my eyes, and immediately the preparation for the work began.

The year itself was one of perfect disaster.

Within weeks of my decision to write for the Lord, my husband was diagnosed with a brain tumor, and within four and one-half months he was dead.

During Stan's final illness, I wrote one more book of the Vampire Chronicles, and a strange book it was. It completed the story of the novel *Blackwood Farm* and closed the Vampire Chronicles as a roman-fleuve, but it also gave voice to my strongest longings to be joined to Christ in a new and complete way.

My hero, the Vampire Lestat, the genderless giant who lived in me, was as always the voice of my soul in this novel, and it is no accident that he begins it with a cry of the heart, "I want to be a saint, I want to save souls by the millions!" Lestat had to tell the truth because I had to tell the truth, and by the end of the novel, confessing his failure ever to be anything but a rambunctious reprobate and Byronic sinner, he nevertheless resigned as the hero of the books which had given him life.

Be gone from me, oh mortals who are pure of heart. Be gone from my thoughts, oh souls that dream great dreams. Be gone from me, all hymns of glory. I am the magnet for the damned. At least for a little while. And then my heart cries out, my heart will not be still, my heart will not give up, my heart will not give in—

—the blood that teaches life will not teach lies, and love becomes again my reprimand, my goad, my song.

And so on the day after my birthday, October 5, 2002, Lestat made his farewell. This character who had been my dark search engine for twenty-seven years would never speak in the old framework again.

And my life as a child of Christ, a writer for Christ, a writer consecrated to Christ, began.

12

IT WASN'T UNTIL THE FALL OF 2005 that I published the first part of my life of Jesus: *Christ the Lord: Out of Egypt*.

From the summer of 2002 through the spring of 2005, my life was consumed with research. I studied not only the ancient historians Philo and Josephus, and all the New Testament scholarship I could lay hands on, but Scripture itself, reading over and over again the Gospels until the language, to which I'd grown so dead in childhood, came alive again, and the vital story of Christ's life flowed through chapter and verse.

Now this was no small feat, coaxing the Gospels to come alive, and it took tremendous dedication; but it was also incredibly rewarding.

It was again a period of relative isolation from contemporary goings-on in Catholicism, and organized religion in general, a period of study that had to do with the New Testament canon and how I might create a probable fictional world for the Christ to whom I was committed body and soul.

My reading skills improved beyond all expectations; I sought days of study without interruption, and finally long nights in which to complete the book in the silence of the sleeping house, with a lone guard on duty to provide meals and coffee for which I barely stopped my work.

Very early on, as I worked on the first book, my commitment was to the orthodox doctrine of the Incarnation, the magnificent love story of God and man which had drawn me back to religion in the first place, the great and beautiful tale of Jesus becoming one of us.

My studies of Jewish life in the first century were also key to my research. I was powerfully influenced by Professor Ellis Rivkin, the Jewish historian, and by others who wrote directly about Jesus as a Jew in a Jewish world.

Essentially, my challenge became a conservative one: to render a convincing portrait of the Jesus of Scripture, the Jesus of tradition, the Jesus of personal devotion and belief.

Only the level of realism in the book was radical. That is, I took the technique of the realistic novel and used it as intimately as possible to present the living Boy Jesus of Scripture with His family, in Egypt, and in Nazareth after His return home. So complete was my commitment to the orthodox doctrine of the Incarnation that no miracle reported in Scripture was left out by me, or skimmed over, or watered down for any contemporary prejudice on the part of "modern" believers who seek to "tame" the power of Scripture in the name of a variety of social concerns.

Jesus is God to me in these pages. Jesus is God to me in my belief. Jesus is God when I pray to Him, and when He answers me. No other "version" of the Man from Galilee has ever held my interest or evoked in me the slightest interest.

It wasn't until February 2007 that the second volume was completed: *Christ the Lord: The Road to Cana*—a story of Our Lord's last winter in Nazareth before His Baptism in the Jordan, His confrontation in the desert with Satan, and His return to Cana for the miracle of water turned into wine.

Once again the commitment to the orthodox dogma of the Incarnation is total. The writings of the great theologians Karl Rahner and Walter Kasper informed and nourished my belief, as did the work of numerous New Testament scholars who do not, in spite of their tremendous range and obvious sophistication, apologize for their own vibrant Christian faith. The numerous books by New Testament skeptics always manage to be helpful, simply because these people ask so many interesting questions. But my answers invariably come out on the side of orthodox faith.

I'm still with the Creed as I say it weekly at Mass; and the "hero" of my new Christian novels is God and Man in the Second Person of the Blessed Trinity, Jesus Christ.

How this has "happened" is not so easy to explain.

It isn't simply a matter of finding skeptical New Testament scholarship so poor, so shallow, so irresponsibly speculative, or so biased. That has indeed been the case. But something else, something infinitely more positive, has been at work in my spiritual journey since 2002—a deepening love of the Incarnation, a deepening meditation on what the whole thing seems to mean.

Now I don't for a moment pretend to be a theologian, and I cannot write with the concise poetic beauty of a Rahner or Kasper, or Joseph Ratzinger, Pope Benedict XVI. No matter how beautiful, theology always ultimately challenges me with its density of abstractions, and sometimes even with its abstract intent.

What I must do here is convey to the general reader—the member of the mainstream who is my brother or sister in the mainstream—how the Incarnation has become the central overwhelming and sustaining mystery of my life.

This morning I was in church talking to the Lord, and thinking about this.

I live in California now.

And I'm miles from the sumptuous and enormous churches of New Orleans that I've described. But the church I go to in California is also an exquisite and uplifting church. One feature it has which is of great meaning to me is a shrine of the Virgin Mary, with a pure white marble statue of Our Lady holding her Infant Son. Nearby is a bank of real wax candles, burning in tiny blue glasses, and before the shrine is a prie-dieu, where one can comfortably kneel, resting one's elbows on the shelf of wood that is part of the kneeler, and pray.

I treasure the time before Mass during which I can come to this shrine and address my special petitions to the Virgin, which are always fervent and gentle and basically have to do with a plea for care. "Take care of me, Mother," is perhaps the most frequent refrain.

What overcame me this morning was a powerful sense of

why the Child Jesus in Mary's arms meant so much to me—why this particular figure of the Lord always touches my heart.

What played out for me was a sense of Our Lord's entire life on earth, and the definite choices He'd made as to His coming and to His time amongst us.

After all, what does the image of this Sacred Child really mean? It means He didn't come down Mt. Sinai as a full-grown male to live out His years of ministry for us and to die for us in Jerusalem. It means that He entered this world through the body of the Virgin Mother, that He came into the world as all of us come, born of woman, tiny, seemingly helpless, and surely obliged to experience life as an infant experiences it, as a child experiences it, taking weeks and months and years before the power of adulthood was within His grasp.

This astonishes me when I think of it, when I really seek to penetrate what it means.

God became a Baby. God became a Child!

His tender little hands and feet, as depicted in the marble statue, don't have the imprint of the redemptive wounds in them. They're seemingly soft and vulnerable and purely innocent. Yet this is God. This is God amongst us. This is God as He was in that mournful Child of the icon, clinging to Our Mother of Perpetual Help.

Why did He do it this way! Think about it. He made the Universe. So He could have done it any way that He liked. He knew what His intentions were. He knew what we were. He knew what He meant to do. Why begin in such complete obscurity and helplessness? Why begin in the arms of a woman who surely had to provide for His every physical need?

I find myself confounded by this, as confounded as I am by the horror of the Crucifixion—that the Lord surrendered to the process of birth and maturation, that He entrusted Himself to the weakness and the inevitable frustrations of a developing little boy.

This is not merely the measure of love, but the measure of an overwhelming affirmation of the human condition. *You have been a child, so I became a child.* That seems to be what the Infant in Mary's arms is saying to me. No wonder He can later say with such conviction in Matthew 18: "Unless you turn and become like children, you will not enter the kingdom of heaven." He had become a child, quite literally and completely, to enter the Kingdom of Humankind.

I found myself dazzled by this as I thought of it this morning. I was dazzled by His long journey from babyhood to manhood, dazzled by the tenderness of those little hands and little feet.

No wonder a great frisson paralyzes me when I look into the Christmas crib, when I hear the phrases of certain old Celtic Christmas hymns. *Sweet little Jesus Boy!*—The Child born in the Manger is more than sentiment and pretty devotion. It's a stark and chilling mystery, this helpless God cradled among animals and fearful humans, a deposit of infinite power in the midst of the age-old stable where man and beast, in the dark dead of winter, have so long found common rest. *The Light shines in the darkness, and the darkness grasps it not.*

How tragic the misunderstanding of modern students of history who snidely declare that Christians coupled the birth of the Christ with an older pagan feast of midwinter in which men and women, full of hope for the return of the warmth of summer, burnt the traditional fires in celebration of the eternal return of life-giving warmth. Christ's birth is the embodiment of this age-old ritual!

It is its fulfillment, and how wise were the church fathers who understood it, and saw the shining Babe as the eternal flame round which generations of pagans had sought a desperate warmth.

I wonder sometimes if there are not Christmas Christians and Passion Christians, and if I have not always been a Christmas Christian, coming closer to the fathomless love of God in His becoming one of us in the Christmas crib. It is not that Our Lord's Passion lacks meaning for me. How could that possibly be? How could I not follow Him to the cross and to the nails and to the spear that pierces His side? This is The Redemption! This is The Atonement! I've already confessed my deep longing for the gift of the Stigmata.

It's only that understanding begins for me in the tableaux of Christmas. A thrilling certainty begins there, in the moment when that Infant is placed in the humble bed of straw. *He died for our sins, yes.* But He was also born for them, nurtured for them, held in His Mother's arms for them, held up by His Mother for us.

Only the God who made the vast reaches of space, its black holes, its sprawling galaxies, its supernova, could have made Himself so small. And what is it we see in that smallness? A child we want to lift to our breast, a child we want to sing to, a child we want to rock in our arms.

What is the word for something so magnificent and so clever, so grand and irresistible? So splendid and so mundane? No wonder that Christmas remains irrepressible, no matter how its critics rise and fall.

And they do come in all guises, from the strict Christians who deplore the hymns in the commercial department stores, to the skeptics who want to ban the Christmas family from secular space. Protestants once banned the medieval Christian pageants; they drove the Holy Family from the church square. Puritans in America went so far as to make the celebration of Christmas illegal. Puritanical secular critics denounce the street decorations that proliferate at Christmas, and the piped-in carols that bring shoppers to the commercial mall.

And yet, as I have suggested earlier, the Christmastime commercial mall is sometimes the only place where one can, in the bustling concrete cities of the modern world, feel the power of the sacred as the old hymns echo and re-echo the shattering sweetness of the original feast.

One has to question the power with which religious puritans and secular puritans try to stamp out all ancient religious feasts in America, how they become bedfellows in their war on Hallowe'en, and their war on Christmas—and how determined they are to rid American experience of the ancient seasonal calendar that once undergirded rural and urban life.

They know not what they do.

Hallowe'en survives with its rich echoes of the Feast of All Souls, and the Feast of All Saints, and is being reconfigured in many places in America; thank Heaven, it refuses to die.

The Holy Family always survives. The Christ Child will not be denied. And everywhere on December 24 and 25, the Child is born again in the midst of inevitable winter darkness and reaches out with warm delicate and curling fingers:

> *A thrill of hope the weary world rejoices*
> *For yonder breaks a new and glorious dawn.*

This is the mystery that rivets me to the heart of Christ. This is one way of talking of the miracle that theologians have written volumes to describe. This is the mystery that drives my life. *You became a child for me, a babe that helpless? What can I do for you?*

This love, this pondering, this obsession with God as a Human Being, has been the fruit of my labors in writing two books dedicated to Christ.

But my education from 2002 on involved not only an obsession with God's mercy and love in the pages of Scripture that I so effortlessly embraced. It also involved many new experiences of what religion meant to people in America, and what the contemporary concerns of my church were.

As I wrote one book and went on to write another, I was in fact traveling two distinct paths. One path was to the Christ Child, but the other path brought me deeper and deeper into the wilderness in which I am still, to some extent, lost.

I3

THE PATH TO CHRIST is the path I wanted to travel from the very beginning. I wanted to understand Scripture, but to put it more humbly, I wanted to know it. And knowing it involved intense rereading of the Gospels and the Epistles and the Acts of the Apostles, and continuous exploration of the Old Testament as well.

I expected to travel this path. I began with so little knowledge of Scripture that it was embarrassing. The Gospels were inert to me. I couldn't tell the voice of one Evangelist from that of another. I didn't know which incidents occurred in Mark, as opposed to Luke; or what was unique to Matthew; or what was so stunningly unique about the Gospel of John.

Also because I'd heard every word of Scripture from the pulpit, it was hard not to skip over the familiar passages as I read, denying myself an experience of the fluid and living Gospel.

Reverend Rick Warren mentions this very problem in *The Purpose Driven Life.* "We *think* we know what a verse says because we have read it or heard it so many times," says Reverend Rick. "Then when we find it quoted in a book, we skim over it and miss the full meaning."

Well, in the first months of 2002, as I began my research, I was skimming the entire Gospel. I had to make myself stop this. I had to read and reread the entire book until I stopped anticipating and jumping, until the flow of the work became as familiar as the individual words.

Scholars played a special role in this, and none more for me than John A. T. Robinson with his book *The Priority of John.*

Reading Robinson feels like sitting by the fire with a brilliant professor and having him discuss with you the things that happen in John's Gospel as real events. Slowly, you come to realize that for Robinson, this is almost like detective work, figuring out what Our Lord chose to do at a specific juncture, or how He responded to something that occurred. Faith in the text is essential to recovering the vibrancy of it. And suddenly, as I was reading Robinson, the Gospel stopped being a passel of quotations, and became a living account.

I crossed some barrier in my studies. I stopped hearing chapter and verse and got caught up in the story, eager to discover what was going to happen next.

Taken again and again to the Old Testament backdrop for the Gospels, I was soon reading the Old Testament books with equal curiosity and vigor, astonished by the distinct voices of the characters, and the wondrously surprising twists and turns of the various accounts. I fell in love with 1 and 2 Samuel, and the exploits of King David. I became entranced with the Book of Jonah, and the Book of Tobit. I began to see everywhere the explosive creativity of the documents I was reading. I began to feel their pulse.

The writings of N. T. Wright brought alive for me the accounts of the Resurrection, and helped me to see them as the record of men and women struggling desperately to describe something for which they had no experience and no words. Christ had risen from the dead.

It wasn't too long at all before I came to see the distinct personality of each Gospel writer, and to reach the inevitable conclusion—in contradiction to much sophisticated scholarship—that the Gospels were indeed first-person witness, and that they contained our earliest and most accurate knowledge of Christ Himself. The novelist in me responded to the internal and effortless unity of each Gospel, the kind of unity that emerges in any heartfelt written account. I'm certainly not alone in this conclusion. Much worthy scholarship supports the same view.

However, an entire generation of New Testament scholars and clergymen has obviously come of age believing the Gospels to be "late date documents," compiled by "communities" of people, who somehow lived in isolation from one another, and apparently made up words for Jesus according to what these communities thought should be made up. Sophisticated explanations are given for this by skeptical critics, but it always comes down to the same thing: they think the Gospels are fictional documents. They think they are collaborative documents. They think they have been heavily edited. They think they must be "edited" again by the modern student as to what is more or less likely to be "historical," if anything in the Gospel is historical at all. It is sad that the influence of these skeptic critics is so widespread.

Not only do I find no evidence for isolated Gospel communities making up documents for their little groups, but I see no evidence of collaborative writing in the Gospels at all. Collaborative documents would never contain so much that is contradictory and surprising and difficult to explain.

On the contrary, the Gospels, once I plunged into them and let them really talk to me, came across as distinct and fascinating original works. Nowhere does one see the "smoothing" of an editor or a group of collaborators. Too many mysteries are woven into the fabric of the work.

Also something else has happened to me in the study of these documents. I find them inexhaustible in a rather mysterious way.

I'm at a loss to explain the manner in which every new examination of the text produces some fresh insight, some new cascade of connections, some astonishing link to another part of the canon, or to the Old Testament backdrop which enfolds the whole.

The interplay of simplicity and complexity seems at times to be beyond human control.

Picking up the Gospel on any given morning is picking up a brand-new book.

There is something so explosive about this body of work

that it not only dwarfs the fragile assumptions of the skeptics, it dissolves them into nothingness.

And at times I have the feeling that I will die, with my face down in one of these books, on the verge of some new and momentous question or insight. In sum, there's no visible bottom to this well of meaning. It's unlike my experience with any other written text.

Frequently, so frequently as to be disconcerting and humbling, I feel myself on the verge of some response to the words that will carry me beyond where reason has led. To say the words are evocative doesn't cover it. The words push one to the brink of mystical realizations. The words never stop inspiring responses that are beyond the words.

Of course I continue to read scholars at every turn, especially those like Raymond E. Brown and C. S. Keener who devote attention to every line of Scripture. The theologian Cardinal Kasper offers powerful illumination. The early Church Fathers often provide keys to the most difficult questions. The whole enterprise is immeasurably huge and thrilling.

And this path, this deliberate path, has led me to affirm the core doctrines of Christianity that were worked out by the Church Fathers in the Nicene Creed and before.

In sum, I am a conservative when it comes to doctrine because this is what I see! This is what I have found in the texts. This is what makes sense to my mind. The novelist in me has found this complex web of truth and meaning in these books when, frankly, I did not expect to find anything so powerful at all.

Now for the behavioral aspect of this path. It is not enough to read Scripture. It is not enough to go over and over the beautiful words and phrases and events of Our Lord's life.

What does it mean to be a child of this Christ of Scripture? What does it mean to be a believer in Him?

As I moved through the writing of *Christ the Lord, Out of Egypt,* I became so wrapped up in the story that I didn't think much about my own personal behavior, about my own attitudes and how they ought to be affected by what I was studying and writing.

Of course I prayed, I studied, I cried. I went to church and I prayed before, during, and after Mass. I talked aloud to Our Lord. I asked for His guidance. My writing could only take me close to Him. There was no other possibility.

But it wasn't until sometime in 2005 that the obvious leapt out at me. The Lord of whom I was writing, the Lord of whom I was reading, was demanding a complete transformation in Him. And that transformation revolved around love.

It is painful to admit that this realization came to me during a television interview at the time that the first novel was published. I was being interviewed by an intelligent man who obviously took my novel very seriously, and he asked, simply enough: "How has returning to Christ actually influenced your life?"

I found myself thinking about this and then answering: "It demands of me that I love people."

This was a turning point, this simple acknowledgment. Because I began then to realize what the message of Christ was for me: to love my friends and to love my enemies. And the mystery was that loving my friends was sometimes harder than loving my enemies. And that if one loved both, completely and sincerely, and if one could convince others to do this as well, one could, theoretically, bring the Kingdom of Heaven to earth.

In the months that followed, I thought a great deal about this commitment to love. I found myself reading the Gospel of Matthew more than the other Gospels. I found myself entranced with the Sermon on the Mount.

And something came clear to me that had never been clear before. Loving our neighbors and our enemies is perhaps the very hardest thing that Christ demands. It's almost impossible to love one's neighbors and enemies. It's almost impossible to feel that degree of total giving to other human beings. To practice the daily love of neighbor and enemy calls into question one's smallest and greatest competitive feelings, one's common angry reactions to slights both great and small. In sum, the will to love all human beings must pervade every thought, word, and deed. One has to love the rude salesclerk, and the foreign enemy of one's country; one has to love those who are "patently wrong" in their judgments of us. One has to love those who despise us openly and write and tell us so by e-mail. One has to love the employee who steals from you, and the murderer excoriated on national television.

My thoughts on this have been slow and continuous. And the more I read the Gospel of Matthew, the more I do see this Gospel as laying out a blueprint for the Kingdom of God on earth.

These meditations have also caused me to evaluate my reflections on my Christian brothers and sisters. Time and again, I've heard people denounce this or that famous minister saying that he preaches "feel-good Christianity," when, in fact, that minister is obviously preaching this earthshaking commitment to love. That minister is trying to show us that this requirement—to love—can bring the Kingdom of Heaven to earth.

I am a baby Christian when it comes to loving. I am just learning. So far were my daily thoughts from loving people that I have a lifelong vocation now before me in learning how to find Christ in every single person whom I meet. Again and again, I fail because of temper and pride. I fail because it is so easy to judge someone else rather than love that person. And I fail because I cannot execute the simplest operations—answering an angry e-mail, for instance—in pure love.

Another thing which has become obvious to me is that we Christians who believe in organized Christianity—whether it's the Catholic Church or the Lutheran Church, or the community of the Amish in Pennsylvania—we Christians of the churches are faced with a near immediate temptation upon conversion to judge other Christians as deficient and missing the point.

We can't give in to this. Yet this temptation will always be there.

The Gospel of Matthew is explicit on our not judging. The Gospel of Matthew tells us *how* to love. The parable of the Prodigal Son in the Gospel of Luke tells us how to love. Jesus at the Last Supper in the Gospel of John tells us

again and again how to love. St. Paul in his magnificent
1 Corinthians tells us how to love.

And yet the temptation to judge never leaves us alone.
Our Christian brothers and sisters question us as to the
integrity of our conversion. They often condemn our
approach to the Lord. They go so far as to tell us we are "not
really saved" because we have not spoken the words they
want to hear us speak. They suggest that our church is perhaps not Christian or is even demonic. They sometimes
accost us on the basis of our political choices.

We have to accept these condemnations. We have to
accept them without complaint. If we do not accept them,
we are lost almost at once in a miserable negotiation with the
Lord's commandments which can swallow the loving heart
completely in what appears to be a Christian vocation but
which is anything but.

The more I study the New Testament, the more I see
the contradictions enshrined within it. But I see something
else there too. We have been a quarreling religion from
the beginning, born out of an earlier quarreling religion—
Judaism—and in a sense the New Testament enshrines us as
such very clearly, with no easy solution as to how we handle
our quarrels or the contradictory passages except that we
must love! The voice of Christ speaks so loudly in the Sermon on the Mount that surely it drowns out those passages
that urge us to condemn or to shun. But how is one to say so
for sure?

To accept the canon means to accept all of the canon. And
that means there will be no easy resolution ever, and that
learning to live with this tension, in love, is what we must do.

This may come across as simplistic. It is not simplistic. It is life changing and endlessly difficult, and the steadfast determination to love is threatened at every moment. We walk a tightrope over a pit of grasping demons when we insist upon love. And sometimes we walk alone.

The truth is, we are never alone, but we are tempted to think we are alone.

The more I study this, the more I listen to people around me talk about their experience with Jesus Christ and with religion, the more I realize as well that what drives people away from Christ is the Christian who does not know how to love. A string of cruel words from a Christian can destroy another Christian.

Over and over again people write to me to explain why they left a church in bitterness and hurt, because of the mercilessness of Christians who made them feel unwelcome, or even told them to go away.

I'm convinced that it takes immense courage to remain in a church where one is surrounded by hostile voices; and yet we must remain in our churches and we must answer hostility with meekness, with gentleness, or simply not answer it at all!

Reverend Rick Warren writes with shining eloquence of this in *The Purpose Driven Life,* this need to love. But many a venerable Catholic theologian has written of the same imperative. The message of Hans Urs Von Balthasar, of Karl Rahner, of Walter Kasper, of St. Augustine, of St. Paul is—to love. The message of St. Francis of Assisi was love.

We have the famous prayer of St. Francis which spells it out beautifully and poetically:

Lord, make me an instrument of
Your peace.
Where there is hatred, let me sow
Love.
Where there is injury, pardon,
Where there is doubt, faith,
Where there is despair, hope,
Where there is darkness, light,
And where there is sadness, joy.
O Divine Master, grant that I may
Not so much seek to be consoled,
As to console;
To be understood, as to understand;
To be loved, as to love;
For it is in giving that we
receive—
It is in pardoning that we are
pardoned;
And it is in dying that we are
born to eternal life.

We kid ourselves if we think this is "feel-good Christianity." This *is* Christianity! If it isn't Christianity, then what can Christianity possibly be? It's the toughest way to live that there is.

Again I see in the Christmas tableaux of the Holy Family the perfect iconography of this love. I see the love of God in the presence of the Christ Child; but I also see in the Virgin Mother, the embodiment of the truth that the conception of the Child Jesus did not involve violence or a proprietary claim on the part of any human being. The Virginity of Mary is not a rejection of sexuality; it is a rejection of violence, a rejection of ownership, a rejection of the social system of the first century in which even a Jewish woman became to some extent the chattel of her husband. The Virgin Mary is a woman who belongs to no man, and only to God.

And we, whether we are male or female, like Mary, belong only to God.

Joseph is the perfect guardian and the perfect witness. He is the man who assumes the responsibilities of fatherhood. But these are seen in their deepest essence, divorced from any claim established by conjugal dominance. They are freely given, these gifts of fatherhood, and therefore they illuminate all fatherhood for all of us—men or women—as they become a parental ideal.

In the Christmas picture of Jesus, Joseph, and Mary, the family transcends the age-old cycle of fertility and death. Each figure is there voluntarily, and therefore symbolically, and allegorically. Each figure speaks of the pure relationship to the Father in Heaven. This is the Family of Love.

No wonder the hymns celebrate this so fiercely through the centuries. *"God rest ye, merry gentlemen, let nothing you dismay. Remember, Christ Our Savior was born on Christmas day."*

Yet the Christ Child will die. He will grow up to die, and to rise again.

From the moment we come to Christ we start negotiating with all this. And to move out of that negotiation and back to the heart of Christ is the hardest thing, I think, for a Christian to do.

Did St. Francis of Assisi know this when he put the babe in the Christmas Crèche at Greccio? Was he not one of the greatest of the Christmas Christians? Did he not give us the Christmas Crèche?

And yet Francis received the shocking and dreadful wounds of the Stigmata. Francis knelt in awe of The Atonement. But Francis was a Christmas Christian first and foremost, perhaps as he reached out his arms to all God's creatures, and all God's creation, and to Christ Himself.

My path leads me deeper and deeper into these mysteries. The powerful inversion of God, the Creator, become human in the body of a babe enthralls me. The complexity of simply loving leaves me stunned.

This path to Christ, this attempt to grasp the multiple meanings of His life and death on earth, had led me to other truths too. It had led me to unspeakable happiness and a sense of belonging for the first time in my life.

But unfortunately, I traveled another path from 2002 to the present and I think it necessary to describe it in brief.

Before I describe that Other Path, I feel I have to say something specific here about sin. I have talked about the Sermon on the Mount, about the great challenge to love, but I have not talked about my own sin.

I know what sin is. I learned very young.

When I was very little, maybe seven years old, I did something that was a sin. I was with a group of children, on our block, playing in the side yard of a house that had a basement and an open basement window. At one point we crowded to the edge of the basement window and looked down into the empty room. The room must have been over eight feet deep. Perhaps it was deeper. There was a little boy crouching next to me at the edge of the window, and I turned to him, and pushed him so that he fell all the way down to the basement floor. I did it for no other reason than to see what would happen. I did it because I felt it was an interesting thing to do.

I will never forget all my life that little boy's scream as he fell, or the utter astonishment on his face as he looked at me, his sheer disbelief that I could have done such a dreadful and cruel thing to him. I knew instantly that it was wrong, what I had done, very wrong. Yet I had done it, and I had done it for the pure thrill of seeing what would happen if I did.

I don't remember any consequences from this. The little boy didn't die, which he might have. He didn't break any bones, which certainly might have happened. And I don't recall anyone calling me to account for it in any way. The boy's brother doubled his fist and threatened me, uttering the words, "If my brother is hurt . . ." but nothing happened after that, as far as I can recall.

I mention it now because I think I knew evil and wrong in that moment. And during my childhood there were other times when I did things that I knew to be clearly wrong.

What I took away from two of those experiences was an understanding of cruelty and meanness.

A third experience, in which I broke into a florist hot-house with two other little children, and stole many valuable orchids, ripping them off their stems, taught me the exhilaration and false sense of power in breaking the law. That "crime" we confessed. My mother called the florist and told him what had happened. He was a kindly man. He came to confront us and found two sobbing little girls clinging to their mother. He did not press our family for restitution, for which I'm grateful to this day.

These acts were wrong. I knew they were wrong almost immediately after they happened, and I made up my mind—for the most part—not to do things like that again.

But these acts revealed to me my own capacity for cruelty and complete disregard of what belongs to others. They reveal to me now the glamour of evil because I have yielded to it in myself.

From them I know sin. I know what it is.

But the sins I committed in far greater number, in frightening number, and for which I feel equal contrition, have mostly involved verbal cruelty—gossip, ridicule, and mean statements made directly to people to hurt their feelings, year in and year out throughout my life. I regret all these sins with my whole soul.

When people refer to me as a "prodigal daughter" because I have given up writing "about vampires and witches," I am confused. I feel no guilt whatsoever for anything I ever wrote. The sincerity of my writings removes them completely from what I hold to be sin. I also feel no real contrition for my years as an atheist, because my departure from the church was not only painful, but also completely sincere.

Sin for me resides in those acts of cruelty both spectacular and small, both deliberate and careless, and always involving the hurt—the real hurt—of another human being.

I myself am haunted by destructive things that were said to me when I was a child, and over the course of my adult life. I can think of something said to me when I was ten years old and feel exquisite pain remembering how humiliated or hurt I felt.

What that means to me, however, is not only that I must forgive each and every instance in which such things happened, but that I must admit that my own words and actions may still be hurting people who can remember them from numberless incidents over sixty-six years. All that gossip, all that criticism, all that spitefulness, all that meanness, all that verbal sparring, all that anger—*all that failure to love.*

I am convinced that cruelty and unkindness are deeply sinful, because I know this sin in myself and the willfulness to commit it. And I say again that Our Lord's words in the Sermon on the Mount demand that we turn from this sin.

To follow Him, I must come to terms with the sin in myself. To write a memoir like this without confessing one's own capacity for sin is something I cannot do.

Think what a beautiful thing it would be if I could take back every unkind word I ever spoke, or every unkind deed I ever did, either deliberately, or accidentally—if I could take back every moment of pain I ever caused another human being.

How can I do this? Only in surrendering this knowledge, this admission, to the mercy of Christ.

Now I can proceed to the story of the Other Path.

14

THE OTHER PATH WAS PERHAPS INEVITABLE for a student of the religious conversion I had experienced. It was a path into the knowledge of the contemporary church, and an exploration of contemporary Christianity. And it was a path into the experience of contemporary Christians in America, Catholic or Protestant, and what their religion meant to them.

I didn't intentionally seek this path, really.

As described, I have a way of working in blissful ignorance of current church history.

So in 2005, when I went on the road to "promote" *Christ the Lord: Out of Egypt,* I knew precious little of what really went on with Christians in the twenty-first century, and precious little of the debates dividing my own church.

Grateful as I was that my church still existed, in much the same form in which I'd left it, and devoted to my writing and theological reflections, I went forth into the world with an ignorance that was not wise.

The first discovery I made was a good one. Americans cared much more about religion than I had been led to believe by cynical friends and critics. I discovered that rank-and-file Americans everywhere wanted to talk about faith and talk from the heart.

As I visited radio programs, both secular and religious, I was surprised by the heat of the interest. National talk show hosts, after the cameras were turned off, would confess that they, too, were believers, that they, too, had undergone a recent conversion, or a faith journey, and the question of how one writes a novel about Jesus Christ according to orthodox belief was hardly academic.

Meanwhile e-mails poured in after my various television appearances. People from all walks of life said, in essence, "Welcome home." Very few questioned my decision to be Catholic. There seemed a common bond shared by Christians of all denominations, and praise for the novel came from Catholics and Protestants alike.

Again and again, readers mentioned that they'd been reluctant to buy a novel "about Jesus" written by a woman associated with "vampire fiction," but they confessed that once having read the novel, they were extremely pleased.

I can't emphasize enough that this was a wonderful discovery. I was aware that faith and politics were hot topics on news shows. But I simply had no idea how many people, of all ages, took their relationship to Jesus Christ intensely seriously. I was confronted by men and women who felt deeply about faith; men seemed at times to be more interested in

Gospel chapter and verse than women, but both were interested in the commitment to Christ and how it could change one's life. Young people also wrote to me about their journeys to faith, and how glad they were to see a known author declaring herself a Christian.

I became convinced that my urban atheist friends were to a great extent out of touch with Christian America. And I became more impatient than ever with the way that network television portrayed people of faith as hypocrites or pompous windbags, or downright fools.

For years, I'd seen Protestant ministers portrayed in this way, and I'd often wondered as to how this affected my Protestant brothers and sisters. Now I was noticing that Catholic priests were negatively portrayed as well. The pedophilia scandal clearly colored these portrayals, but at the root, there was the old Hollywood skepticism of the man or woman of faith, and a certain Hollywood arrogance that malignant portrayals of Christians were entirely acceptable to American audiences.

Even in my atheist days, I had resented this cavalier treatment of people of faith. After all, I'd lived for nearly thirty-eight years in two worlds—the world of San Francisco and Berkeley liberalism, and the back-home world of relatives in New Orleans and Texas. I'd been deeply and silently offended by the Hollywood assumption that believers were stupid, or lying about their beliefs.

Now as a believer, I experienced an even greater skepticism about these routine television portrayals. And the question plagued me: if we are a nation of churchgoing Christians—and other fervent believers, including Jews, Buddhists, and Muslims—why does television not reflect this fact? Why does television seem to say the opposite, that we are a nation of skeptics bedeviled by a few noisy bothersome political Christian fools?

I haven't found a satisfactory answer to my questions. I do know, from personal experience with network executives, that serious Christian programming is not something these people want to touch. Though the nightly crime shows might ridicule ministers and priests, the networks fear the power of the Christian audience to reject a Christian program with e-mail campaigns, boycotts, and jammed fax machines. As a consequence the negative portrayal of the individual Christian seems to be the norm on national television. And there is a total vacuum when it comes to faith-based programming. Motion picture studios seem equally leery of anything that might arouse a Christian backlash. Yet films contain the same negative picture of ministers and priests.

My opinion is that most network and studio executives don't really understand the Christians of America. They have been powerfully impressed with the success of Mel Gibson's *The Passion of the Christ,* but they don't really understand why this film was a success. And they know that they themselves cannot replicate Gibson's success. As a consequence, though they talk about tapping into the Christian audience, and developing more Christian programming, they are confused as to what to do, and what might offend Christians or what Christians might want.

Recent political involvement on the part of certain Christian denominations has further complicated the picture for people in the entertainment business, just as it has drawn criticism from some secular groups.

I cannot recall a time in America when there has been more talk of religion and politics. But I've also noted that many Christians have become disillusioned with overt political involvement and are reconsidering the meaning of separation of church and state.

The heat of the religious debate on political issues, and the number of books published today on the subject—all this speaks to me of the importance of faith in people's lives. Even the most strident critics of political religious groups are often high-principled individuals who care very much about how a good and fruitful life is lived.

But to return to my travels through Christian America, I found something else besides faith.

I found controversy and division within religion itself. I encountered it in the most casual of ways.

I hadn't thought it radical, for instance, for a deeply orthodox Catholic to hope for the eventual ordination of women. Or for a Catholic to believe that our gay Christian brothers and sisters would soon be accepted into the fold. I hadn't thought it radical to suggest that all churches would soon be more accepting of unconventional behavior involving sex.

But these did prove to be radical suggestions. And I soon learned that the Body of Christ is deeply divided on matters of sex and gender.

I have found these same divisions in Protestant Christianity as well as Catholic—congregations strongly against "feminism" and gays, and other congregations far more accepting, and embattled, on the issues of women's ministry or the right of gays to worship within the church.

Sex is an obsession of contemporary Christianity, even more now perhaps than it was in 1960 when I left my church.

In the face of all the reading material on these questions, I have to remind myself of my central vocation. It is not to learn church history or to become involved with church politics. It is not to discover the reasons for the widespread pedophilia scandal, or even to discover why so many clergymen chose to break their vows, not with consenting adults, but with adolescents and children. It is not to change the churches of others, or the church to which I belong. All of these matters must be left for others.

My vocation is to write for Jesus Christ.

It is to belong completely to the Man at the Top.

That means a fidelity to the Jesus of Scripture, the Jesus of the Four Gospels, and it means that I must never bend, in my portrayal of Him or His followers to any attempt to retroject my current values on the past.

If one becomes too involved with doctrinal arguments and sexual and gender controversies, one can be alienated from the Lord.

I can't allow that to happen.

I'm too keenly aware that, in 1960, my agonies as a Catholic became intermingled with questions of pure faith; and, leaving my church, I left the Lord.

So, though I am again and again confronted with the political problems of organized religion, I strive mightily to ignore them.

The Lord Jesus Christ is where my focus belongs. And my commitment to Christ must remain unchanged.

And I know something now which I didn't know when I was eighteen years old, something which the intense study of Scripture continues to reinforce: the politics of religion has almost nothing to do with the biblical Christ.

Try as I might, I can find *nothing in Holy Scripture* that supports this contemporary obsession with sex and gender on the part of our conservative churches. In fact, the more I study Scripture, the more amazed I am to discover that Jesus Christ Himself cared nothing about gender at all. Over and over the Gospels reveal Jesus treating men and women equally, and indeed insisting upon their equality. The ways in which Jesus approaches women, instructs them, works miracles for them, reveals His identity to them, and uses females and female imagery in His parables makes it abundantly clear that Jesus came to save women as well as men.

The New Testament scholar Ben Witherington III studies these questions in great and satisfying detail in his *Women and the Genesis of Christianity.* Let me quote one passage: "Thus, the community of Jesus, both before and after Easter, granted women *together* with men (not segregated from men as in some pagan cults) an equal right to participate fully in the family of faith." Other scholars have come to similar well-documented and well-explained conclusions.

And I would go so far as to say that the Old Testament too reveals an astonishing number of vibrant and forceful women who play key roles in the stories that we hold to be the foundation of our faith.

Here, for me the two paths—one into the study of the Scripture, and the other into the state of contemporary religion—reveal an immense divide.

The more I study the Lord's words, the more assured I am that He is the transcendent God who compelled love and devotion from me before I even began the intense study of the sacred texts.

When I go to accounts of the Lord's Supper, I find there no division, but only the unifying power of the Eucharist. Christ gave His Body and Blood to me. He gave it to you.

But one does not have to read the scholars to understand this equality of men and women in the New Testament. It is easy enough for the conscientious reader to discover on her own. Jesus' conversation with the Samaritan woman at the well is a marvelous example of the Lord's invitation to a woman to become His disciple. It is her "testimony" that brings her villagers to Jesus. And on perhaps the busiest day of Our Lord's life, the day of His Resurrection, He stopped near the empty tomb to comfort Mary Magdalene as she wept. In that tenderest of moments, *He called her by name.* The early church did not hesitate to declare Mary Magdalene "the Apostle to the Apostles." One has to wonder, how is it that two thousand years later, our churches are arguing about the roles of men and women with such venom and such heat?

I think that—to find the origin of conservative religion's obsession with reproductive rights, and gender roles, one has to look not to the Bible, but to the detailed and responsible histories we have of marriage as an institution, and its evolving meaning over the centuries. And plenty of these books now exist. Histories of private life, histories of childhood, histories of women and the changing roles of women, histories of the institution of marriage—all of these shed light on the culture's inevitable preoccupation with gender and sex and family. And these studies also affirm that we are in the midst of such incredible experiment and change that scholars can scarcely remain current.

No wonder churches seeking to affirm an immutable doctrine about gender roles find themselves frustrated, and frustrating.

Predictions as to the fate of homosexuals in our society, predictions as to the reconfiguring of the family, predictions as to the role of women in politics and religion, predictions as to developing sexual ethics—these are almost impossible to make.

All around me, I see people, single and married, gay and straight, having children and loving those children, coping with the demands of parenthood and the economic demands of changing conditions, and persevering as people have persevered throughout history, to make families and to be in families, no matter how the economic and social ground shifts beneath their feet. I see the childless gay couple and the childless straight couple seeking to establish households in which stability, fidelity and love are paramount.

It gives me hope to see this throughout America, and to see it in an America that is *not* a post-Christian nation, but a nation hungering for the teachings and the presence and the grace of Our Lord Jesus Christ. It is a Judeo-Christian nation, encompassing Buddhists and Muslims who share the same irrepressible belief in a Creator or a Greater Good beyond themselves. It is a nation of secular humanists who care as passionately about the rights of individuals as do their religious brothers and sisters. It is a nation of 12-step programs in which the belief in a Higher Power nourishes the believers with incalculable strength.

These truths I celebrate with my whole soul.

I do not want to be tempted by divisions and controversies. I do not want to judge, to condemn, to quarrel. I want to remain with the Lord on the green grass of the hills of Galilee as He gives us the blueprint for God's Kingdom on earth. I see Him standing there in His simple, timeless robes, with His arms out. I hear His voice as if He were only a few feet away. I draw closer to Him, until I am sitting at His feet. Centuries don't matter anymore. He is as real and immediate now as He was two thousand years ago. Having entered history, He remains our own and our timeless God. I feel that I can reach out and silently touch the hem of His robe. I close my eyes as I listen to Him, and I dare to imagine on my head, on my shoulder, the warmth of His loving hand.

But I say to you, love your enemies, and pray for those who persecute you, that you may be children of your heavenly Father, for He makes His sun rise on the bad and the good, and causes rain to fall on the just and the unjust.

How can this not be enough?

How is it that I, unlike Him, am a broken creature of my time? And in the softest voice possible, want to say this:

Centuries ago the stars were sacred. A man could be burnt at the stake for declaring that the earth revolved around the sun. Churchmen feared that if astronomers gained authority over the Heavens, Scripture would be undermined.

But no such thing took place. Scripture is too great, too powerful, too fathomless for such a thing to take place.

Now the Christian world holds the stars to be secular.

Most of the Christian world holds biology and geology to be secular as well. And Scripture is as potent and irresistible as ever. Scripture still guides our lives.

And the stars are still the lamps of Heaven.

Is it not possible for us to do with gender, sexuality, and reproduction what was long ago done with the stars? To realize that these are also secular areas, and that new sources of information about them may be as valid as the information given us long ago by men who gazed through the first telescopes at the night sky?

Is it not possible that gender, sexuality, and reproduction are areas for which the Ten Commandments and the Sermon on the Mount may be entirely adequate as they are for every other sort of behavior we face?

If I am wrong on this, I pray you will forgive me for this suggestion. And a suggestion is all that it is.

But I see people driven away from churches by these issues. And some for their whole lives.

And too many make the mistake I made. They leave the loving figure of Jesus Christ because they feel they have to leave His churches.

I will never leave Him again, no matter what the scandals or the quarrels of His church on earth, and I will not leave His church either.

Next Sunday, I will walk into my parish church as I do every week, and I will celebrate the Mass with my fellow Catholics, and I will stand before the altar of the Lord.

This is a California church, as I've already mentioned—very different from those ornate and immense churches of my youth. It was built only a few short decades ago, yet it reflects the ancient truths and dogmas of my venerable religion as beautifully as did the churches in which I grew up.

And coincidentally, beyond the altar, there stands against the curving wall of the sanctuary that very same giant statue—of the Crucified Christ embracing St. Francis with His right arm—that so startled me in a church in Brazil over ten years ago, and that so captivated me in a little shop in San Francisco ten years before that.

Yes, in this church, of St. Francis of Assisi, here in the Coachella Valley of California, I stumbled upon that very same image. And it means to me what it has always meant: The Lord loves us. The Lord embraces us. The Lord has made this world for us. And from the scandal of the cross, He reaches down to embrace His beloved saint—the saint who put the Infant Jesus in the crib at Greccio, the saint who bears the wounds of the Stigmata in his uplifted hands.

I am broken, flawed, committed: a Christmas Christian searching for that Stigmata, for the imprint of those Wounds on my heart and my soul, and my daily life.

Printed in the United States
by Baker & Taylor Publisher Services